Is There a P

The Life Story and Thoughts of Dorothy Stolzenbach Payne

As told to Virginia McNeil

Revised and Expanded by Rebecca Payne Shockley

Dedication by Dorothy S. Payne, 1985:

To my three children, who are finding as much happiness in the musical profession as their father and I did, and to many, many friends in the Keyboard Club.

Table of Contents

Title Page	
Dedication	ii
Table of Contents	iii
Preface and Acknowledgments by Rebecca Shockley	viii
Preface to 2nd Edition by Karl Payne	xi
Preface by Virginia McNeil	xii
Introduction by Virginia McNeil	xiii
Dorothy Stolzenbach Payne (Boris Goldenberg Photo)	xv

PART I: THROUGH THE YEARS WITH MUSIC	**1**
My Early Years in Lima and Pittsburgh	**1**
My College Years	**4**
A great loss	4
Albino Gorno	5
I join the CSO	6
I meet Karl Payne	7
Graduation, A New Job, and Marriage	**9**
Karl Joins WLW	11
I meet Percy Grainger	11
The 1930s	**14**
Soloist with the Symphony	14
Joy Followed by Sorrow	15
We Become Parents	15
I Leave the College & Establish My Own Studio	16

The Start of The Keyboard Club	17
Study with Joseph Lhevinne	18
Study with Harold Bauer	19

The 1940s — 19

We Move to Clifton	19
Our Second Child	20
I meet Claudio Arrau	20
A Request from Percy Grainger	21
We Need a Larger House	21
Our Third Child	23

The 1950s — 24

Karl Joins the Symphony	24
A visit from Alexander Tcherepnin	24
Study with Vronsky and Babin	25
A Choice - Symphony or Teaching	26
My First Trip to Europe	26
Summer Activities with the Keyboarders	30

The 1960s — 30

Performing Bach Triple Concerto with the CSO	30
A Serious Illness	31
Accompanying Blanche Thebom	31
Karl's Illness	32
Honorary Degree	32

The 1970s — 33

A Family Program	33
A Master Class by Byron Janis	33
My London Recital	34

Chamber Music	34
The First Payne Family Concert	35
Soloist with the Cincinnati Chamber Orchestra	35
"Women of the Year"	35

The 1980s 36
    A Smaller Home 36
    A Second London Recital? 37

Our Children as Adults 38
    Dorothy Katherine 38
    Karl, Jr. 39
    Becky 41

PART II: THE KEYBOARD CLUB 44
    The Start of the Club 44
    A Concert featuring Eugene Goossens 45
    The Warriors with Grainger and Goossens .. 45
    Our Monster Concert 45
    The Keyboard Club Scholarship Fund 48
    Keyboard Club Special Programs 48
    The Dorothy Payne Piano Project 49
    Two Concerts by Percy Grainger (1948 and 1950) 49
    Photos from Grainger's 1950 Visit 51
    Two Keyboard Clubs – and a 25th Anniversary 52
    Grainger's Last Visit 52
    My First Trip to Europe 53
    "Piano Camp" for Keyboarders 53
    A Memorable Keyboard Club Concert 55
    A Halloween Party and Other Oddities 56
    The Keyboard Club's European Trip 57

House Tours	75
Vronsky and Babin Concert & Master Classes	76
The Payne Family Concerts	76
Recitals, Workshops, and Meetings	78

PART III: RELECTIONS ON MUSIC AND PIANO TEACHING — 80

The Musical Amateurs - God Bless Them	82
Children's Practice	85
Group Lessons	90
Individual Lessons	93
From Generation to Generation	94
Every Pianist a Good Sight Reader	97
The Adult Beginner	99
Art is Long - and Difficult	102
The Many Moods of Music	104

PART IV: POSTLUDE — 108

Reflections by Rebecca Shockley

APPENDIX I: DOROTHY PAYNE AS TEACHER — 111

Teaching Style and Philosophy	111
Group Classes for Musicianship	111
Posters of Musical Terms	112
The Key Signature Carousel	114

APPENDIX II: SELECTED PROGRAMS AND LETTERS — 115

1918 Recital by Dorothy Stolzenbach (age 14)	115
1926 Recital by Dorothy Stolzenbach and Karl Payne	116

1926 Graduating Class, College of Music	118
1934 Master's Degree, Cincinnati Conservatory	119
1948 Recital by Percy Grainger	120
1950 Recital by Percy Grainger	123
1958 Recital by Percy Grainger	126
1971 London Recital by Dorothy Payne	129
1930 Recital by Dorothy Payne, Canton Oh	131
1932 Recital by Louis Kohnop	132
Programs from College Years (1923-1927)	133
Letter from Eugene Goossens, 1936	134
Transcribed	135
Letter from Percy Grainger, 1959	136
Transcribed	138

APPENDIX III: SELECTED PHOTOS   139

Dorothy Payne in 1930, 1934, 1946	139
Dorothy in home studio, 1967, 1970	140
Keyboard Club meeting, c. 1970	141
Vronsky and Babin	141
Vronsky and Babin Masterclass, 1969	142
Payne Family Photos	143
Performers in Keyboard Club Recitals, 2002, 2017	147
Dorothy Payne at 1984 May Festival Opening	148

Preface and Acknowledgments by Rebecca Shockley

A few years ago a friend suggested that I should consider preparing a revised edition of this book. The original 1985 edition was re-printed in 2010 with minor additions, but all the copies are gone. Over the years my mother's story has been read and loved by many people, especially those who knew her, studied with her, or whose children and/or parents also studied with her. But others who never knew her also seemed to find it fascinating, and I sensed there was a potential audience for this story – especially among piano teachers and students.

As I re-read the book, I was struck again at just how extraordinary she was. Her story was still compelling, but I knew that she had forgotten some things by the time the book was completed. I also knew that my father, who was an excellent writer, had helped her edit the early parts of the book. But after his untimely death in 1967, she had to complete the work without his help, which made it more difficult.

In this edition I have made the following changes:

1) Fixed little typos and other mistakes.

2) Updated the look and feel of the book, as much has changed since the primitive word processing available in 1985.

3) Taken out redundancies and fixed awkward sentences.

4) Added anecdotes and missing information about important events in her life.

5) Updated information about our family.

6) Clarified the organization of the book by making the section on the Keyboard Club into a separate chapter, and added subheadings to making it easier to find information.

7) Added many new photos, integrating as many as possible into the text.

8) Added three Appendices:
Appendix I. DOROTHY PAYNE AS TEACHER
Appendix II. SELECTED RECITAL PROGRAMS (performances by Percy Grainger, Dorothy Payne and others).
Appendix III. SELECTED PHOTOS

9) Added a *Postlude* covering her final years and beyond.

To try to preserve the basic flow of the story, I am using a different font for my additions:

I have used *italics* to indicate material I have added to the original text.

I am forever grateful to Virginia McNeil, a longtime student of my mother and devoted member of the Keyboard Club, for her foresight, determination, and the many hours of hard work she spent producing the first edition of this book. Without her efforts, much of my mother's amazing life story and remarkable legacy might never have been documented. I owe thanks as well to her husband, Dave McNeil, for editing and proofreading the manuscript, and to Ranald West and Russ

Ahlbrand for their assistance with the first edition. In addition, I owe special thanks to my brother, Karl Payne, for checking the original manuscript and re-issuing the book for the 75th anniversary celebration of the Keyboard Club in 2010. Karl has also been a source of some great stories and anecdotes from my mother's life, and he and his wife, Susan Rivers Payne, have provided valuable letters, photographs, and other materials to help me fill in parts of the story.

I owe special thanks to my longtime friend Michelle Conda, Professor of Piano at the University of Cincinnati College-Conservatory of Music, for first suggesting this project to me. Her enthusiastic encouragement and guidance, superb editorial skills, mastery of technology, passion for teaching, and fascination with my mother's life story, have made her an ideal partner in this endeavor. I could never have done it without her help.

Rebecca Shockley

Preface to the 2nd edition by Karl Payne, Jr.

"Is There A Piano In The House?" was first published in 1985 on the occasion of the 50th anniversary of the Keyboard Club. This printing coincides with the club's 75th anniversary. During the past 25 years much has happened, including the passing of my mother, Dorothy Stolzenbach Payne in 1992, and my beloved sister, Dorothy Katherine Payne, in 2010.

A concert series sponsored by the Keyboard Club honoring my mother was started in 1993. The programs have featured the three of us – Dorothy, Becky, and myself - as well as other fine pianists, most of whom have had a connection with her.

During the last twenty years the club has sponsored a piano scholarship program for high school students who study with members, and also provides ongoing support for piano study for children and adults at the Peaselee Neighborhood Center in the Over-The-Rhine area of Cincinnati.

One of Mother's special qualities was her willingness to accept students of any age, regardless of their ability. She felt that everybody could benefit from music study and was always willing to fit as many students into her schedule as time would permit. Such a policy was rare for a first-rate performing artist who was also a personal friend of many of the world's great pianists and conductors.

It is the professed aim of the Keyboard Club to promote the same spirit of community and love of good music that Mother epitomized in her life's work.

Preface to the First Edition by Virginia McNeil

"Dorothy," I said at the end of one of my piano lessons, "Anyone who has lived as interesting and beautiful a life as you have ought to write a book about it."

"I've been told that I should," she said, "but how would I find the time?"

Before the conversation ended, we set up times for me to come with notebook and tape recorder. We were well along the way when Dorothy went on a trip, then I went on a trip and somehow the project was shelved.

With the 50th anniversary of the Keyboard Club coming up we thought the time had come to get at the project again.

Dorothy's activities have been written up in newspaper articles from time to time, but to have her tell about these activities and embellish them with her personal anecdotes made these sessions something very special.

I hope those of you who read this book will get as much pleasure as I did from helping with it.

Introduction by Virginia McNeil

I first met Dorothy Payne when I was looking for a piano teacher for my 7-year old daughter, Lois. A friend said, "Why don't you take her to Dorothy Payne? You might as well go to the best Cincinnati has to offer." I told her I thought I'd give Mrs. Payne a call. She said, "Naturally you'll call her Mrs. Payne when you first call her, but before long you'll be calling her 'Dorothy' like everyone else does."

After the first lesson Dorothy assigned Lois to be the 4th student in one of her groups. Lois loved it. Because mothers brought their children from long distances, they usually came in and waited until the lesson was over. Dorothy's living room on Terrace Ave. was an interesting one in which to wait, as the walls were full of pictures of famous musicians and pictures of her own family members. In front of each of the two large overstuffed couches on which the mothers usually sat was a coffee table laden with books and magazines, some for adults and some for children. By reading books from her coffee table I was introduced to many interesting biographies of musicians. Of course, most mothers managed to keep an ear tuned to what was going on in those very fascinating classes. When the lesson was over each student was offered a candy bar from the big basket on the table.

Periodically Dorothy would have a class session for many students. Then the mothers would sit in the big reception hall and be the audience. I'll never forget the first Christmas class I attended with Lois. A fire was blazing in the fireplace, the house was decorated for Christmas, and the children were asked to play the carols they had learned. Playing with them on his violin was her husband, Karl Payne. There was something very touching about hearing the gorgeous violin music of a symphony player being accompanied by these 7- and 8-year-olds. The sessions always ended with refreshments to which the children looked forward.

When I heard that Dorothy taught adults, I signed up, and before long I became a member of the Keyboard Club. What joy that has been through the years.

Since I taught piano, I was invited to attend the Keyboard Teacher's meetings, where teachers could exchange ideas, discuss materials, and receive the benefits of Dorothy's great teaching ideas. These valuable meetings were always followed by lunch in her large, comfortable dining room.

I had the honor and privilege of serving as president of the Keyboard Club (morning group) and was delighted that during my tenure we sponsored the first Payne Family Concert and celebrated the 40th Anniversary of the club.

Through the years Dorothy has touched the lives of many, many people. Each has an individual story to tell about becoming acquainted with such a remarkable woman.

I'm sure I echo the thoughts of many when I say that friendship with Dorothy has been one of life's great blessings.

Dorothy Stolzenbach Payne

PART I – THROUGH THE YEARS WITH MUSIC

My Early Years in Lima and Pittsburgh

I was born in Lima, Ohio in 1904. My father, Jacob N. Stolzenbach, and my mother, Cora Bostaph Stolzenbach, were extremely devoted. My brother, Fred, and my sister, Margaret, were older than I, so there wasn't much conflict between us. Ours was a very happy home life.

Mother loved music. She both played and sang very well but she never learned to read music. When she thought that both Fred and Margaret were old enough she sent them to a teacher for music lessons.
Unfortunately they were not interested. My sister always said that in five years she learned to play one piece, and that not very well.

Dorothy Stolzenbach at age 3

When, between two and three years of age, I started crawling up to the piano and picking out things that I had heard her sing or play, my mother immediately thought I must have some talent. When I was about six years old she sent me to a teacher who told my mother that I would never learn to read music because it was easier for me to get someone to play a piece first and then I could reproduce it.

My mother then tried another teacher whose lessons were equally unproductive. Since mother was not easily daunted she tried one other, which was as dismal a failure as the first two. Even mother was about ready to give up by then.

At about that time my father was transferred to Pittsburgh to take charge of the Frigidaire office there, one of the first in the country. He had many headaches with the first Frigidaires, but he stuck it out for quite a while.

In Pittsburgh Mother found a former school friend of hers who was teaching piano. Mother explained the problem she was having with her youngest daughter who, by that time, was nine years old. This friend was a dear person and an excellent teacher. Her name was Mrs. Henderson. I'll never know how, but she did succeed in teaching me to read. It opened up a whole new world and music became a great adventure from then on. Her daughter, Elizabeth, was about my age. In a few years we played duets together, gave recitals together, and became good friends. I admired her very much and wanted to read like she did, for she was an excellent reader.

Dorothy in high school

There was a very fine teacher in charge of music at my high school in Pittsburgh. Every year she put on a musical such as *The Mikado* or *Robin Hood* and I was asked to accompany. At that school they had chapel every morning and I was expected to play a very short solo and occasionally accompany singers. Therefore I had to learn to read very quickly. It was a very valuable experience, which I thoroughly appreciated when later on in life I studied with Percy Grainger. I was very happy in the high school in Pittsburgh.

After a few years, however, my father decided to go back to Lima and enter the real estate business with his sister. This move was very hard for me. My brother and sister were by that time both in college, so the move didn't matter as much to them, but for me to leave all my friends and all my musical acquaintances when I was a senior was very difficult.

When we became settled back in Lima I found a very fine piano teacher there by the name of Mrs. Harry MacDonald. A former student of William Mason in Chicago, she was a fine organist and pianist and took a great interest in me. She kept telling me and my family that I must go on in music. My mother was especially interested, and I think my father felt that if my mother thought it was good for me it was all right with him. They always told me that when I was a little girl I used to sit with them in church before I went to Sunday school, and when he would sing the hymns I would cry. They didn't think it was an emotional disturbance on my part; it was just the fact that my father sang out of tune.

He was willing for me to go on with musical studies, but told Mrs. MacDonald that there wasn't much money. She told my father that she had a friend who was, coincidentally, a former friend of my father, who was coming to visit in the spring in order to see her mother who lived in Lima. This friend's name was Mrs. Adolph Hahn. She taught at the College of Music in Cincinnati where her husband was the director. Mrs. MacDonald arranged for me to play for her. I was a bit nervous, but I usually like to play for people, so it didn't bother me too much. At the end of my playing Mrs. Hahn said, "Dorothy, I think you must come to Cincinnati, for you have really outstanding talent. I can't promise, but I think there is every reason to believe you could win a scholarship at the College of Music." What joy! We figured that with the scholarship, my father's help, and a loan from my sister we could manage.

One unusually warm day in December we went to Cincinnati and stayed at the famous old Grand Hotel near the railroad station down near the river. The hotel is no longer there, but it had been the scene of many well-known balls and parties, and many renowned people had stayed there. I was quite impressed. When we went up to the College the next morning I was even more impressed, for there was a feeling of warmth and friendliness about the old building. There I played the pieces that were requested, and the next day Mrs. Hahn told me that I had won a scholarship with full tuition. We were delighted. I also met Mr. Hahn, who was a charming person.

Dorothy in college

The Hahns were always interested in me all the years I was there. I felt they were my friends, and I spent many happy hours at their home. My move into the dormitory was the beginning of a whole new life.

My College Years

A great loss. During my first year at the college I had a very great sorrow when my mother had an operation for an embolism and lived only four days. She was only 46 years old. This was difficult for me and tragic for my father, as my sister was teaching out of town at the time and he was very lonely.

Albino Gorno. I dearly loved my music classes, especially my piano lessons. I studied with Dr. Albino Gorno, who was the head of the piano department. He was a marvelous Italian pianist who had come to this country as Adelina Patti's accompanist. He liked it here and decided to stay. When the Cincinnati Symphony gave its first performance of the famous Tchaikovsky Piano Concerto, Gorno was the soloist. People who heard it told me it was a great performance, but unfortunately he got so terribly nervous when he played that he decided he would like teaching better, so he never played in public again. We who studied with him were privileged to hear him. He was a great musician and had a wide knowledge of all kinds of music. He was very demanding and many times would spend an entire lesson on two or three measures. Then he would explain, "I'm not talking about just these measures, but any measures that are similar."

Albino Gorno

He never praised anyone. Sometimes at the end of a recital, or if we had played with the orchestra, he was known to mutter, "Better next time." That was the nearest he ever came to a compliment, and we knew that his allowing us to play in public was a sign that it wasn't too bad. This was hard to get used to, and though very deflating for me, it was probably what I needed at that point. He was basically a kindly man, but oh, how excited he became, sometimes even screaming and throwing things.

He was a great believer in the modern music being written at that time, and was one of the first teachers who had his students study Gershwin's *Rhapsody in Blue*, which then was not accepted by everyone. He thought it was a great work.

Music to him was so important that he worked with it all the time. He was always arranging things for two pianos. His manuscripts were dreadful to read, but we did learn to do it, and it was a fine experience to learn to play a modern piece for two pianos, and then on one piano. That way we learned so much more about the harmonic structure. He also insisted on our studying the analysis of a piece. At first he was talking about things that were way beyond me, but under his instruction I began to understand harmonic structures long before I encountered them in harmony class. He felt that no one was a good musician who did not understand the harmonic structure of a work. He had his students do a lot of ensemble work – two-piano music, chamber music, and eventually concertos with the orchestra.

How well I remember the great thrill I had in my junior year when I played the first movement of the Tchaikovsky *Concerto* with the college orchestra. It was so exciting to hear the sound of the orchestra all around me and to feel that I was a part of it.

I join the CSO. During my senior year I became assistant pianist with the Cincinnati Symphony Orchestra, which was a whole new world. The first pianist was also new to this job, though she was older than I and a more experienced musically. We were both very green and laughed afterwards about how we looked at the first parts we had to play and neither of us knew what "tacit" meant.

Fritz Reiner

Fritz Reiner was the conductor then, and though he was a very difficult man, I admired him, for he was a great musician.

In November 1927, she performed the first movement of Rachmaninoff's second concerto with the college orchestra.

I meet Karl Payne. During my first year Mr. Hahn asked me if I would accompany one of his violin students, Karl Payne, and since I did a lot of accompanying I was willing. I think Mr. Hahn had ideas then - I never really knew, and he never said - but he was very eager for us to play together. One thing led to another. Soon we were rehearsing long and often, and romance blossomed. Karl was an extraordinary person. He was a fine musician with high ideals, worked very hard, and had about the most fantastic sense of humor of anyone I have ever known. I could write a book about his antics, for which he was known throughout the school.

Karl Payne ca. 1926

I remember one instance in harmony class. Dr. Durst, our teacher, felt Karl had great ability and allowed him to come to any theory class that he wanted. Of course, he always managed to come to the ones I was attending. In one class there was a young man who was not very talented but was extremely conceited. He was sure he would become the next great American composer. In this particular class he was at the piano, playing one of his works alongside Dr. Durst. Neither the "great one" nor Dr. Durst noticed (of course the class did) that while they were playing, Karl had appropriated some of his music and very quickly added some sharps, flats and naturals in odd places all over a page or two of the manuscript. The "great one" finished his first piece and came back to get his next composition (the one Karl had "fixed"). He started to play it, and you never heard such a mish-mash of sound. He kept muttering, "I don't understand, it didn't sound like this when I played it before. I don't know what's the matter." The class was simply convulsed but no one said a word. I don't know whether it ever took him down any, but he was totally mystified, and I'm sure he never really discovered what had happened.

After we had been playing together for some time, Karl introduced me to his parents. His mother was a vivacious woman with a great sense of humor and great determination. She loved music although she was not very musical herself.

Karl's father, a large gentleman, was very musical. He played violin, guitar, mandolin, and double bass. When he was in the army he organized an orchestra that played at special functions. He gave Karl violin lessons and was, in fact, his only teacher until he enrolled at the College. As much as his father liked music, he didn't want his son to become a musician, but Karl liked music so much that he decided to audition for a scholarship at the College and was delighted when it was awarded to him. Every day he used to walk from their home in Newport, Kentucky, to the College - a distance of four miles - in order to save transportation costs.

One summer during our courtship days, Karl went to Mt. Eagle, a summer camp in Tennessee, to play in their orchestra. We had very lengthy correspondences, as he was a most interesting letter writer. One week after I didn't get a letter and was really worried, I wrote that I expected more letters, and asked if anything was the matter? Within a few days I received six letters one day, five post cards the next, and four letters the third day. The mailman would look at me, shake his head and smile. I never again reproved Karl for not writing.

Graduation, A New Job, and Marriage

After I received my degree, I began teaching at the College of Music because I'd felt drawn into it. I was concerned that perhaps I shouldn't start to teach at the same place I had studied, but Mr. Hahn prevailed upon me, and Karl, I knew, wanted me to stay. As I started to teach, I didn't feel very well equipped and I don't suppose I was a very good teacher, but I learned by doing and became quite involved in teaching. Suddenly, about the second year, I began to realize that there was a great challenge in getting people to make music, to love music, and to improve them as much as a student can be improved. To really make music becomes a way of life. Teaching music draws one very close to people. One can never be very remote and just give piano lessons; it involves their whole lives. This gradually came to me, and then I worried about people who didn't have much money and had to make great sacrifices in order to give their children music lessons.

Dr. Gorno didn't teach young students, so he would send them to me. I had some very talented ones - in fact, some of my most talented students. During the years I taught at the college I had three pupils who soloed at the young people's concerts with the Cincinnati Symphony. This was a source of great joy to me.

Karl and I wanted to be married. We didn't have much money, but we thought we had enough. We were both teaching at the College of Music, and Karl was also playing at the Lyric, a movie theatre with

Engagement, 1927

an orchestra. When we had enough money saved we set the date - August 1, 1928.

We were married at my home in Lima, Ohio. The wedding went very well, even though it was 97° in the shade and long before the days of air conditioning.

For our honeymoon we accepted an invitation from the Wilsons to visit their lovely summer home on Martha's Vineyard, where they had spent many summers. George Wilson was the president of the College of Music and a fine man. Since neither of us had ever been east, we traveled to Boston first, stayed there a few days, and then went on to Martha's Vineyard, that lovely spot. The ocean was so beautiful, the house very old, and they had Portuguese servants. What a great experience for us.

Karl and Dorothy on their Honeymoon 1928

How well I remember one day when we went out on their son-in-law's yacht. It was a sailboat with a motor and could be used either way. Karl kept looking at me anxiously wondering how I felt. The sea was a little rough, but I insisted that I felt fine, which I did, and I was enjoying it. We had been out a little while when someone in the party passed around a box of cookies. I took one and then happened to look at Karl. He had a very greenish look on his face. He refused the cookies and was not very happy the rest of the trip, and he was more than glad to get off the boat. But in spite of the seasick episode, the trip to Martha's Vineyard was a very lovely way for us to begin our married life.

When we set up housekeeping we had very little furniture, but one thing we had to have was a piano. The best we could manage was an old upright, which received plenty of use. We lived in an apartment on McGregor St. in Cincinnati for about four years.

Karl joins WLW. *In 1929 my father joined the WLW Radio Orchestra, a position he held for 20 years. He would have preferred playing in the Symphony, but in those days orchestra musicians were not paid very well, so he felt he could better support a family at WLW.*

WLW Radio Orchestra 1929

I meet Percy Grainger

When we had been married for a little over a year, I went to Chicago and auditioned for a scholarship to study with Percy Grainger, the famous pianist who had been born in Australia, studied in Germany, became famous in London, and later became an American citizen. I had heard him play in Cincinnati. He played the organ transcription of the Bach *G minor Fantasy and Fugue*, and I thought I had never

Percy Grainger, 1930

heard such beautiful Bach. It was so well played with all the voices so clear. I was determined to study with him.

He was a most dynamic man and very kind. Each applicant had to play for him, first sight reading something and then playing something especially prepared for the occasion. To my great delight I was awarded one of the scholarships, which entitled me to a private lesson a week with him and the privilege of attending every class he taught. Then I decided I wanted an extra lesson per week for which I was willing to pay.

Percy Grainger was interesting in every way. He was a vegetarian, and I think we all tried a vegetarian diet because he had such dynamic vigor. Everything he did he did with intensity.

When he first came to the Chicago Musical College, a room had been booked for him in the hotel across the street. His studio was at least eight floors up. They showed him his studio and told him his room was in the hotel across the street. He said, "What do I need that for?" They said, "Well, you do have to sleep." He said, "Yes, but I sleep on the floor. I don't need that room." He slept under the piano!

When he would return to his studio after having been outdoors, he would walk up the eight flights of stairs to his studio, sometimes even carrying a piano bench on his shoulder. He would not think of taking an elevator. He was small in stature but he did all he could to develop strength. He wouldn't own an automobile because that kept him from walking. In fact he never owned a car in his whole life.

Grainger Class, Chicago, 1930
Dorothy in the front row, far left

He and his wife, Ella, were married in the Hollywood Bowl, and for a honeymoon they took a long hiking trip. Fortunately she liked to do the same things he did, so they had a very happy marriage. She understood his idiosyncrasies and could accept them. She said to me one day in her Swedish accent, "I find Percy difficult at times, but he's never boring." That was true. He might have been difficult in the things he demanded of people but he definitely was never boring.

They used the hotel room when Ella came to visit. Students enjoyed having her come. She came to all the classes and was just as absorbed in them as he was. It didn't matter whether it was 8 a.m. or 10 p.m., there was the same feeling of excitement. We played chamber music and two-piano music in the evenings, and it was a summer full of wonderful experiences.

When I first started studying with Mr. Grainger, he asked me with whom I had been studying. When I told him Dr. Gorno was the only artist teacher I'd ever had, he said he was amazed at how well prepared I was. I was certainly grateful for Dr. Gorno's lessons.

Mr. Grainger was an entirely different personality from Dr. Gorno. He let his students play through pieces and then demonstrated and went over them very carefully. After he found out how well I could sight read and the manner in which I had developed it, he gave me all sorts of extra lessons. Karl came up one time during the summer and met Mr. and Mrs. Grainger. He was as impressed as I. I always felt that when I came back to Cincinnati I wasn't quite the same. I had new ideas, especially about group teaching, that Mr. Grainger thought were very good, and certain ways of studying and approaching compositions. He admonished his students never to become static; he certainly never did. Working with him was very productive and very exciting. I went back to teaching with my head full of new ideas, which I was eager to try out.

Through the years Mother continued to study with Grainger every time she could, attending his summer classes in Chicago, at Interlochen, and at New York University. They became close friends, and she regularly invited him to Cincinnati to stay in our home while giving master classes for her students and a public recital (in which my mother and her students also performed.) She also visited Percy and Ella several times at their home in White Plains, where she and Percy would rehearse together.

The 1930s
Soloist with the Symphony.
Shortly after Eugene Goossens became the director of the Cincinnati Symphony in 1931, he came to the College of Music to audition members of the senior piano faculty to play a solo with the orchestra. As a junior faculty member, I was not

Eugene Goossens, 1942

permitted to audition for him. Mr. Goossens didn't choose anyone on this visit, but asked to return later and hear some other pianists. I was then permitted to audition, and was chosen to play the Liszt-Busoni *Spanish Rhapsody* with the orchestra. I shall never forget it. I had played with the college orchestra, and I had been a part of the Cincinnati Symphony, but I had never experienced the thrill of being a soloist with a great symphony orchestra. It was one of my life's great joys.

Joy Followed by Sorrow. About two weeks after I had the thrill of soloing with the symphony my father died, and a few months later Karl's father died. Karl's mother grew very lonely, so we moved into her home in Newport to be with her. We sold our old upright piano and used the piano that she had.

In 1932, my mother received a Master of Music from the Cincinnati Conservatory of Music. She also became an excellent organist, and held regular church positions for many years, notably at Mt. Auburn Baptist Church, which housed a very fine organ.

Dorothy Katherine, 1937

We Become Parents. In 1935, while we were living with Karl's mother in Newport, our first child was born, and we named her Dorothy Katherine.

She was a delightful child and we always enjoyed her. Before she was two she was trying to pick things out on the organ at a friend's home. Then she tried picking out tunes on our piano. Music drew her like a magnet. She particularly loved Bach, and tried to pick out his music. I remember one time when she was about two she wanted me to play something and so I started to play "Mary

Had a Little Lamb." She said, "Don't want 'Mary Had a Little Lamb,' want Rachmaninoff." (Of course she used her own two-year-old's pronunciation). I learned then not to play down to her. She wanted the best of all kinds of music and could reproduce just about anything by ear, which was fantastic. I began to think, "There I see myself again, playing by ear." But at that point I felt it hadn't hurt me, and I still think that.

At first she was a slower reader than other students – even though she had fine facility – but when her reading finally caught up with her playing she went very fast.

I Leave the College and Establish My Own Studio. As the years went on Mr. Hahn was not well. He retired from his work at the College of Music and Mrs. Hahn also left. This was difficult for me, as I had always been so close to them and felt they were a part of my life. When the new regime started, I didn't feel I belonged in the same way. I was anxious to experiment with new ideas in teaching, many of which I had learned while studying with Mr. Grainger, but I wasn't always permitted to do this. I was told I was a younger teacher and I should bide my time. I couldn't have students appear with the college orchestra because I wasn't an "artist teacher," even though three of my students had performed with the Cincinnati Symphony. Certain things seemed to me to be unjust and wrong, and I became increasingly unhappy, but Karl, as well as many others, advised me to stay on.

I thought of setting up my own studio. I knew it was very difficult to have any kind of prestige as a private teacher, but I just couldn't see going on the way I was. So, after worrying about it for several years and becoming increasingly more unhappy, Karl and I both decided that the time had come for me to leave the College. The board of directors tried to persuade me to stay, but I had made up my mind.

In 1934 I established a studio in downtown Cincinnati at 220 E. 4th St. above the Baldwin Piano Co., and the move turned out to be the right one. Some of my students stayed with me and I began to get others. I liked being able to manage my own affairs and being free to experiment. I felt if I had an idea I should try it, and I'd soon know if it was good or not. If not, I could discard it, but if the idea proved to be good I would continue to use it. I tried many interesting experiments, and most of them, I will say, have proven through the years to be successful.

The Start of the Keyboard Club. My teaching schedule and home duties were keeping me very busy, but I loved every minute of it. I taught many children as well as a number of adults. I realized that adults who are not professional musicians seldom work the compositions they are learning up to a performance level. I felt what was needed was an opportunity for these adults to perform. So in 1935 I got together with eight of my students and we played for each other. We enjoyed it so much that we decided to meet at each other's homes once a month. We decided to call our group "The Keyboard Club." It kept on growing, and over the years the Keyboarders had many interesting experiences, which are described in Part II of this book. Little did we know what a long, happy and fruitful association it would be.

Keyboard Club, 1939

Study with Joseph Lhévinne. *In 1937, Mother drove to Chicago to attend a master class by renowned pianist Josef Lhévinne. After hearing her play, he agreed to give her a private lesson for $30, which lasted two hours, and which she found very valuable. In a letter to my father, she wrote that he complimented her "fine fingers and arms, and splendid sense of rhythm and musicality." He also gave her tips on "arm weight, technique, phrasing, wrist position, color, and pedaling." She found his ideas on technique different from Grainger's but his musical ideas similar, and described him as "very exacting but kind."*

Later that summer, she drove to Interlochen for more Grainger classes. She described having to play marimba and xylophone (including several glissandos!) in the percussion group for a concert there, and she found it rather fun. But she said Percy was so exhausted the following day that he fell asleep during her private lesson, so she waited five minutes until he woke up, after which the lesson resumed.

Study with Harold Bauer. In 1939, Mother traveled to Boston to play in master classes by British pianist Harold Bauer. He had been highly recommended to her by Grainger, who considered him an expert on French music. She found the classes very inspiring, and described him as having "none of Percy's eccentricities but many of his ideas." She marveled at his musical memory, noting that "no one has played any part of anything that he cannot play without notes," and found his ideas on Bach and Mozart in relation to their instruments very enlightening. Hearing him refer to "my friend de Pachmann," "my friend Godowski," or "my friend Debussy," made her aware that Bauer was "one of the elect, despite his very modest and kindly manner."

Harold Bauer

The 1940s

We Move to Clifton. Since Karl's mother was becoming more reconciled and adjusted after the death of her husband, we decided that it would be wise to move to the Ohio side of the river, since both Karl and I had all our activities in Cincinnati. Karl had terminated his work at the College of Music and had taken a job as violinist in the WLW radio studio orchestra. In 1940 we found a small house on Lorraine Ave. in the Clifton neighborhood of Cincinnati, which was large enough to accommodate the two grand pianos I had in the downtown studio. I therefore closed the downtown studio and had my studio at home. I shall never forget one boy who was determined to be the very first student to take a lesson in my home.

Grandma missed Dorothy Katherine, so little Dorothy spent a considerable amount of time visiting her Grandma, who spoiled her as grandmas have a way of doing, but I'm sure those visits were good for both of them.

Our second child. In 1940, when Dorothy Katherine was five years old, we were blessed with the birth of a son whom we named Karl. As he was growing up he was a thin child and we thought he wasn't as robust as he should be, but from the time he had his tonsils out he proved to be very robust and had a great zest for things. He was always a very happy boy. When Karl was about three, I can remember his picking out some tunes on the piano. One was "Mary Had a Little Lamb", another was a Christmas carol, and the third was a part of a Brahms piece. Even at that age he had varied interests.

Mother, Karl and Dorothy K., 1940

I meet Claudio Arrau. When Claudio Arrau, the famous Chilean pianist, came to play with the Cincinnati Symphony, I was fortunate to be able to meet him through the Hahns. He agreed to hear me play, after which he

Claudio Arrau, 1941

invited me to be in a class he was organizing in New York.

I was excitedly making plans to go when he contacted me to say that because of changes in some of his concert plans he could not proceed with the class. This was a big disappointment for me, but when he came to Cincinnati after that he always got in touch with me and the Keyboarders. In fact, he referred to the Keyboarders as "my girls." We always considered him a good friend.

Claudio Arrau, 1963

A Request from Percy Grainger. In November 1943, my mother received a letter from Percy Grainger, informing her that he had just been hired to perform Gershwin's Concerto in F with the Indianapolis Symphony in 10 days. He loved the piece but had never played it, and needed to rehearse it before the concert. He proposed stopping in Cincinnati for a few days on his way to Indianapolis, so that he could rehearse it with her and also to practice with a "gramophone recording" – if she could arrange that. I am sure she was thrilled at the request, but in a subsequent letter he told her that the concert had been postponed until December, so I assume the rehearsal never took place.

We Need a Larger House. We seemed to be bursting at the seams in the house on Lorraine Ave., and we also felt the time had come when Karl's mother should move in with us. The problem was we had to find a house suitable to have her with us and large enough to accommodate our two grand pianos. I had always admired the large dark red brick house at the corner of Whitfield and Terrace in Clifton. It had a large wrap around veranda and just had a homey look to me. In 1945 I contacted a real estate agent that we knew and asked if by any chance he could find out if that house was for sale. He checked and told us that it was. He arranged the sale and sold our house on Lorraine.

The new house was perfect for our needs. There was a large entrance hall, which opened into a very large living room with a wood-burning fireplace. I saw immediately that two grand pianos could easily fit there. At the end of the living room was a double door entrance into a very large dining room, and the kitchen could be entered from either the hall or the dining room. Almost at the end of the large entrance hall was a beautiful stairway leading to the upper floor.

On this floor there were three ample sized bedrooms suitable for our family, plus a fourth room with a private lavatory which opened onto a little porch - just perfect for Karl's mother. It would give her the privacy she wanted, but she could still be with us. I thought it would be good to have a piano in Dorothy Katherine's room, so we put a used upright in there.

Moving day came, one of those hot Cincinnati summer days. I thought I had everything marked exactly as to where it should go but by the time the movers hauled everything in I said, "Just put it any where." The neighbors' eyes were bulging, watching three pianos being moved in. Things were really in disarray. Little five-year-old Karl looked at all the confusion and said, "I don't like it here; I want to go home." I had to tell him that this was now home. Ten-year-old Dorothy Katherine looked at the crystal chandelier in the living room with wonder and said with a smile on her face, "We're rich at last!" We gradually got things settled and the house served us well for many years. Lessons, classes, recitals, luncheons, teachers' meetings, guests - the house accommodated them all. It was truly a house of music.

Our Third Child. After a few months in the new house, we were blessed with the birth of a second daughter. We named her Rebecca but always called her Becky. She seemed to know from the first that it was music she wanted.

Payne Family, 1946

When Mr. Grainger would come to Cincinnati to play with the Symphony he would come a few days early and stay a few days longer if he had the time. He would stay at our house and give master classes, which were always a source of inspiration. I remember when Becky was two she had heard me and another pianist playing a two-piano arrangement of Bach's *Little Organ Fugue in G minor*. This apparently fascinated her. She managed to pick out the subject and the answer up to the entrance of the third voice in the proper key. She was playing this one day when Mr. Grainger walked into the room and expressed amazement. She looked at him and said, "That is a 'Bafume.'" Even though she couldn't say "Bach Fugue" she knew what it was. He was very intrigued with that and with all of the children's musical talent. I've always been glad that they were old enough to remember him, and to have known his dear wife, Ella, as well.

In 1947, Mother traveled to New York and attended a lecture on the piano music of Hindemith by the renowned pianist and teacher, Olga Samaroff, with illustrations by her students. Louis Kohnop, who had studied with Mother as a youngster, was a student of Samaroff's at Juilliard.

The 1950s

Karl's mother lived with us on Terrace Ave. for about five years until she died of a stroke. We all missed her a great deal.

Karl Joins the Symphony. Karl had worked at WLW Radio for 20 years when they decided to discontinue their studio orchestra. Life changes. The day of the disc jockey was arriving and studio orchestras were becoming too expensive. Karl had always wanted to play in the Cincinnati Symphony (which was directed by Thor Johnson at that time), so he took a year off for extensive practice before auditioning. He was very happy when he was accepted as a member, and he knew that his mother would have been very happy with that move, for she had always encouraged him in all his musical endeavors.

Karl and Dorothy, 1955

A Visit from Alexander Tcherepnin. In 1953, Mother wrote to the Russian composer Alexander Tcherepnin (then teaching composition at DePaul University in Chicago) to come to Cincinnati to give master classes for her students. He stayed in our home for three days and gave several classes focusing on 20th c. music. He wrote a beautiful letter (excerpted below) expressing his admiration for her teaching:

"What has touched me the most at your home is precisely this climate of love for music, this deeply human approach to it...that you communicate to your students... whatever will be the future of your students...all of them will love and consider music; your effort, your energy, will never be in vain."

Alexander Tcherpnin, 1953

Study with Vronsky and Babin.

Our children were growing up. After two years as a piano major at Miami University in Oxford, Ohio, Dorothy Katherine transferred to the Eastman School of Music in Rochester, N.Y. For her graduation gift we gave her a trip to Aspen, Colorado. Her unselfish father decided we should both go. There we coached with the famous duo piano team of Vronsky and Babin. Mr. Babin did most of the teaching, and Vitya, his wife, added valuable comments. They worked as a team in both teaching and performing.

Vronsky and Babin Class, Aspen, 1956

Mother continued to study with by Vronsky and Babin over the years, traveling to the Cleveland Institute or Northwestern University to attend their classes, and inviting them to Cincinnati to give classes for her students. After Victor's death in 1972, Vitya gave several more classes in Cincinnati.

Babin Class, 1960s

A Choice - Symphony or Teaching. Those were busy years. Playing in the symphony, teaching, and home duties made a very full schedule. The Symphony seemed to be playing more and more modern things, which required a great deal of practice. It came to a point where I had to make the choice - either symphony or teaching. I loved the Cincinnati Symphony and found it thrilling to be part of a big orchestra and hear all the other instruments around me. I learned the precision of rhythm. There was so much that I learned from that experience, and yet I knew within my heart that teaching was my life. So in 1957 I decided to devote all my energies, after caring for my family, to teaching.

I have never regretted my decision. And in 1962 I had the privilege and honor of serving as Honorary President of the Women's Symphony Committee.

Honorary President, Women's Symphony Committee

My First Trip to Europe. In 1957 Dorothy Katherine received a scholarship from the Three Arts Club of Cincinnati, which supports young women in the arts, enabling her to study in Vienna. I wanted very much to visit her, as I had never been to Europe, but it seemed like such an expensive undertaking. I wanted to go at the end of her first year, but I just didn't think I could do it.

My devoted Keyboard friends, unbeknownst to me, decided that they would start a fund for my trip. If anyone says that a woman can't keep a secret, I can quote this incident as proof that she can.

Over a hundred women were working at this, contacting all the members, and keeping an account of the money that was collected and how much I would need for such a trip. One night I came home from a performance. Suddenly the front door was flung open by my husband and I saw a sea of very happy faces shouting "Surprise!"

I went into the dining room, and there was a lovely spread and a huge cake with the words "Bon Voyage." The Keyboarders then handed me a check, which covered my entire expenses for the trip.

Could anyone have more loyal friends, and could anyone have been more delighted? I'm sure the answer is no. Karl had known about it, but he too had kept silent, and he was as thrilled as I was.

On April 18, 1958, I sailed on the *America* on one of its final voyages to Europe. We had rough weather, but I was a good sailor. The ship arrived in Bremen and Dorothy was waiting for me at the port. It was a happy reunion. We spent the night there and then took the train to Vienna the next day. She had learned to speak German very well. I was constantly amazed at her asking questions and conversing with Germans as if she had lived there all her life. I was not as fortunate.

We arrived in Vienna and went to the home of her dear landlady, Frau Schleifer, who spoke no English, and I spoke no German. Dorothy had taught Frau Schleifer's little five-year-old daughter, Renee, to say "Die Mutter aus Amerika." She greeted me with this, but my German wasn't equal to a reply. However we seemed to communicate. It was such a lovely place and we had a fun time. Dorothy's friend, Cynthia, a cello player, was living at the same place. We had a gay whirl in Vienna - the opera, concerts, visits to Schubert's home, to places where Beethoven had lived, places where great musicians were buried and all the beautiful castles - all these things together made Vienna a never-to-be forgotten city.

After Vienna we went through the lovely Alpine country down into Salzburg and Innsbruck. The scenery there is simply magnificent. I shall always remember it. Though I've been there since, it seems to me that the first impression was the most spectacular. I couldn't believe it was so lovely, and the people were so friendly. Of course, it was a help that Dorothy could speak German.

We then went into Switzerland and down into Italy. Neither of us spoke any Italian. All either of us knew were the musical terms, and they didn't come into very much use during the day. We found the people to be most helpful and kind. We loved Italy. We went to Milan and saw the marvelous La Scala Opera House, where we heard a performance of *Madame Butterfly*. Dorothy and I had both heard it before. We are both sentimental, and in the last act, when the heroine commits suicide, we cried as always. I know it's going to happen, but I always cry, so we sat there sobbing. When the lights went up, we were so ashamed of our red noses and faces that we just cowered in our seats until most of the audience had gone. Then, holding handkerchiefs to our faces, we went out and hoped nobody noticed us too much. But it was a wonderful evening.

Next we went to Florence and heard some beautiful concerts in the great castles there. It was part of their summer festival, and we loved the city. Then we went to Rome.

We always felt that the Italian people were so kind, and we had one instance of it on the train from Milan to Rome. We got on a very crowded train, as most Italian trains are, with five pieces of luggage. There were two gentlemen in the compartment where we chose to sit. One had on the uniform of the Italian Army. They helped us arrange our five bags and we settled down for the ride. Then the conductor came through to check tickets.

**Mother and Dorothy K.
Italy, 1958**

When he looked at ours he said something in Italian, which we, of course, could not understand. One of the men, who spoke some English, explained that we were in the wrong section of the train. This part of the train would be put off somewhere else and would not go on to Rome.

We looked at him with looks that said, "What do we do now?" He said, "Stay here. I'll find you some seats." It seems that he had been in England after the war and spoke very fluent

English. After he had been gone about ten minutes he came back and said, "We'll go now." The two men moved our luggage for us, and we didn't have to do a thing. When we got several cars ahead he had seats for us. We thanked him and he very smilingly departed. We happened to look out into the corridor where we saw two Italian privates who had been ousted from their seats by our friend who was an officer. They smiled at us and didn't seem to mind standing for the rest of the trip. This was one example of their kindness, which we found to be apparent everywhere.

There is so much music in Italy, which we dearly loved. In Rome we heard some very fine concerts. The whole trip was a great pleasure. I shall always remember my first European trip with much happiness. We had sent letters to the Keyboarders along the way to let them know what happiness their generosity had provided, and some of these letters were published in the Cincinnati *Enquirer*. As much as we enjoyed every minute, we were happy to get home again and tell all our friends about our trip.

Summer Activities with the Keyboarders. I had some wonderful summer adventures with members of the Keyboard Club, including a 2-week "piano camp" in Michigan in 1959, and a tour of European music festivals in 1962. Both are described in detail in Part II.

The 1960s

Performing the Bach Triple Concerto. In February, 1960, the Cincinnati Symphony Orchestra programmed Bach's *Concerto No. 2 in C Major* for three pianos and string orchestra. Max Rudolph, the new conductor, gave me the honor and privilege

Max Rudolf, 1960

of being one of the three pianists. The other two were the Rev. John Reinke of Xavier University and Babette Effron, the symphony pianist. It was difficult finding a space to rehearse the three piano parts together, so a friend offered us an upright that she no longer needed in her home. It was delivered to my living room studio, and there it stayed for many years! Keyboarders helped swell the audience, and the concert was a great success. (In March of that year the Keyboard Club had a dinner meeting, with Max Rudolph as guest speaker.)

A Serious Illness In 1963 I discovered I am not indestructible, for I was hospitalized for several months with acute bacterial endocarditis (inflammation of the lining of the heart). Being hospitalized was certainly a new experience for me, but with the love and good wishes of my family and friends, I responded to the expert medical care and was gradually able to resume my teaching schedule again. (But my doctor made me promise to quit teaching on Sunday afternoons!)

While in the hospital, Mother received cards and flowers from many friends and colleagues both near and far. These included a dozen red roses from pianist Rudolf Serkin, whose master classes she had attended in the summer of 1960 at Marlboro.

__Accompanying Blanche Thebom.__ In 1964 Mother accompanied a recital by renowned mezzo-soprano Blanche Thebom of the Metropolitan Opera for the Artist Series at the College of Mt. St. Joseph. An autographed photo of the singer as Cherubino hung on our living room wall for many years.

Blanche Thebom

Karl's Illness. In the mid 1960s, Karl's health began to fail. It wasn't easy to watch him go downhill. The doctor finally told us that he had terminal cancer. That was a most difficult period of my life, watching the life forces of the person I so dearly loved ebb away. He passed away in 1967. My Keyboard friends, families of my students, and other friends were all most understanding. In his funeral sermon, Dr. Netting of the Clifton Presbyterian Church spoke of how much joy Karl had brought into the lives of others with his music and his pleasant personality. I think everyone who attended that service felt the same way, especially his own family.

I wondered how I could go on, but I knew I would, since God always gives us strength somehow. I knew I must continue teaching; that was now more important than ever. Keyboard Club was also very important, for I regard each Keyboarder as a special friend.

Honorary Degree. Somehow sorrows and joys have a way of being balanced in life. Before Karl died, I received word that at the dedication of its new College-Conservatory facility later that year, the University of Cincinnati wished to confer on me the honorary degree of "Doctor of Humanities." That was a very great honor indeed. Dr. Walter Langsam, whom I always admired greatly, was the president of the University at that time. Five honorary degrees were awarded at that ceremony. The recipients included myself and Louise Nippert, a longtime patron of the arts, for contributions made to the cultural life of Cincinnati. Honorary degrees were also granted to Norman Dello Joio, George Balanchine, and Metropolitan Opera tenor John Alexander, so I certainly felt I was in good company, and a composition by Norman Della Joio commissioned for the occasion was performed. It was amazing to think that just doing what I thought ought to be done day after day would lead to such an honor.

Dorothy Payne (3rd from left) receiving Honorary Doctorate, 1967

The 1970s

A Family Program. In 1970 Dorothy Katherine, Karl and I were asked by the Music Department of the Cincinnati Woman's Club to present a program for their meeting in April of 1971. Becky was away at the time and unable to join us, but we had a wonderful time doing it.

Making a recording of that program was our first such experience. Since I had joined the Musicians' Union when I played for the symphony, I had to get permission from them in order to make the recording, and it was readily granted.

Byron Janis Master Class. *In 1970 Karl drove Mother to Tanglewood, where they attended a master class by Byron Janis. Karl remembers that one student was performing a Mozart concerto but had no accompanist. When Janis asked for a volunteer to accompany her, Mother agreed to sightread* the orchestra part. After she finished, Janis commented, "Very fine reading!"

My London Recital. In 1971 I was invited by Ella Grainger and Stewart Manville, archivist of the Grainger Library Society, to play a program in London's Purcell Room. I played many of Grainger's own compositions which I had studied with him, as well as some Bach, Chopin, Byrd, Debussy, Ravel, and Grieg, all of which I had studied with him. The society is devoted to furthering the performance of Grainger's music and is really doing a fine job in keeping alive the memory of this great man. I gave a preview of the concert at the Cincinnati Woman's Club before leaving for London. A recording was made of that concert and the records were sold by the Keyboard Club. Since Becky and John were then living in Richmond, Indiana, where John was teaching at Earlham College, Becky was able to drive to Cincinnati on weekends to teach a number of my students during the three weeks that I was away.

***Chamber Music.**
Mother continued to perform regularly for clubs and in homes in Cincinnati, and playing chamber music gave her great pleasure. She had wanted to become a professional accompanist, but was told in college that women could not do this, since wearing a dress onstage would distract from the soloist! But she collaborated with other musicians whenever the opportunity arose.*

With Erik Kahlson and Arthur Bowen, retired CSO players, 1970s

The First Payne Family Concert. In 1974 the Keyboard Club asked if the four of us would present a Payne Family Concert. We had given a program for the Woman's Club in 1971, but this was to be a full-fledged concert. This concert, which took place that November, and the two others that followed, are described in Part II, The Keyboard Club.

Soloist with the Cincinnati Chamber Orchestra. In April 1977, Mother performed Beethoven's First Piano Concerto with the Cincinnati Chamber Orchestra. The concertmaster was Jorja Fleezanis, a fine violinist, who went on to become concertmaster of the San Francisco Symphony and later the Minnesota Orchestra. Jorja also performed with Mother in a Mozart piano quartet for a house concert in 1979.

"Women of the Year." In 1979 I felt very honored to be chosen as one of the "Women of the Year" by the Cincinnati *Enquirer*. People from all over the city write in to the paper to nominate their choice and give reasons for their nomination. The *Enquirer* selects twelve women each year from those nominated. In addition to the activities of the nominee, the number and quality of the letters has great influence on the committee. I'm sure my Keyboard friends banded together and told other friends to write in. It is quite an honor. Each day for twelve days, one of the women has her picture in the paper along with an article describing her activities and why she was chosen to be a "Woman of the Year." On the day of the awards, there is a big luncheon at a downtown hotel. The women being honored are seated at the speaker's table and each is asked to rise in turn as a brief account of her activities is given. Many Keyboarders attended

Cincinnati Enquirer Women of the Year

the luncheon. On this occasion, too, I felt I was in good company, as one of the other women selected that year was the mother of James Levine, Director of the Metropolitan Opera.

The 1980s

A Smaller Home. By 1980, my children felt that since they were all living out of town, the house on Terrace Ave. was too big for me to care for by myself. They found a nice little house nearby on Howell Ave.

Duets with Karl Jr., 1980

It wasn't easy to leave the old house, which held so many memories, and such a large collection of musical instruments. With my children's help I made the move. They worked out a place for all my files of music, and I was able to bring two grand pianos with me. I had to find room for all my pictures, the most important being pictures of members of our family. There were pictures of Bach, Beethoven, and Rachmaninoff, plus autographed photos of Dohnanyi, Tcherepnin, Curzon, Max Rudolph (under whose direction I had performed with the Cincinnati Symphony), Shostakovich (who sat behind us at a concert in Edinborough and autographed our programs), Vronsky and Babin (whom I first met in Aspen and who later gave a concert and classes for our Keyboard Club), Claudio Arrau (with whom I almost studied), and of course, my close friend Percy Grainger. When the living room wall became filled with pictures, we used the stairwell in the hall for more.

With my two pianos, my music, and my pictures, I have been very comfortable in the house at 585 Howell.

Today I keep up with my teaching, and although my schedule is not as strenuous as before, I enjoy it as much as ever, and Keyboard Club is still important.

Through the years I had been active in several other clubs: Music Lovers, which I joined before I was married; Matinée Musicale (both associate and active groups); MacDowell Society; and the Clifton Music Club, as well as the Cincinnati Woman's Club. I have thoroughly enjoyed my association with all these groups and attend as many of their meetings as time will permit.

For the past four years I have spent a month in London, Edinburgh, and the Dartington Festival in the summer, and I am looking forward to going again this year. With three children launched on musical careers I couldn't ask for more.

Mother visited the Dartington Festival in 1979, where she heard a performance and an exciting class by French pianist Vlado Perlemutter (who had played for Fauré). She particularly enjoyed master classes by pianist Alfred Brendel at Dartington. Karl accompanied her on her last trip abroad in 1986, which included London, Oxford, Edinburgh, and Paris.

A second London Recital? *In 1982, Mother again flew to London at the invitation of the Percy Grainger Library Society to plan and begin rehearsing for a second recital there. She had a productive visit, but unfortunately on the way home she fell and broke her arm in JFK airport. She flew home in pain and was met at the airport by kind friends who drove her to the hospital. She made a good recovery and continued to teach and give informal performances, but the concert had to be cancelled. Nevertheless, she still loved England, and made regular trips back with Dorothy Katherine or Karl until 1986.*

Our Children as Adults

Dorothy Katherine. After graduating from Eastman, Dorothy spent a year in Cincinnati teaching piano at a private school and serving as organist at a local church. We converted Becky's bedroom into an upstairs studio and equipped it with an old grand piano so she could practice there. (Karl, Sr. also used it to teach his violin and beginning piano students.) Dorothy Katherine then received a scholarship from the Three Arts Club to study in Vienna for a year (which was later extended for a second year). It was during that time that, through the generosity of my Keyboard friends, I was able to enjoy my first trip to Europe.

When she returned, she taught at Pacific Lutheran University in Tacoma, Washington, for six years before returning to Eastman for graduate studies, where she also served as a theory instructor at the school and organist at a local Lutheran church. There she met William Penn, a composer on the faculty with a specialty in film and theater music. While teaching there she completed her Ph.D. in music theory, after which she and Bill were married. We performed one of Bill's compositions, *Miroirs*, at our Payne Family Concert in 1974. In 1985, She and Bill moved to Austin to teach at the University of Texas. There she collaborated with her colleague, Stefan Kostka, in publishing *Tonal Harmony*, which became the most widely used college theory text in the U.S.

DKP, University of South Carolina, 1994

Dorothy later became a music administrator, serving as Chair of the music departments at the University of Connecticut and

Arizona, and Dean of the College of Music at the University of South Carolina. There she had the pleasure of conferring an Honorary Doctorate on Marian McPartland. In Columbia she continued to teach undergraduate theory, which she dearly loved, and served as a Lutheran church organist. When her health declined, she retired to Cincinnati to live with Karl and his wife Susan. She died there in 2010 of Parkinson's disease.

With Marian McPartland

Karl, Jr. Karl played the piano some as he was going through school, but when he was in high school he said, "I don't want to be a professional musician. I like music, but just as a hobby." We got him a clarinet and a saxophone, which he enjoyed, although he still played the piano occasionally.

When he graduated from high school he decided to major in electrical engineering, so he went to the University of Cincinnati and was doing very well. In his second year, however, he came to me one evening and said, "Mom, I miss music. I didn't know it meant so much to me, but I'm away from it too much, and when I sit in a class of calculus I almost get sick because I'm not at the piano." I had noticed that he had been coming home at noon to practice and wanting to go to symphony concerts, which he never did before. Suddenly music was vital to him. His father and I discussed it and wondered what we should do. It was hard because he hadn't had a particularly good background. He hadn't studied all the standard things. He just liked to play. We talked it over with him, trying to point out that it was a very precarious life, and that as an engineer he had a better chance of a very good job when he came out of school. He would have to start from way back if he wanted to major in piano because his background was very haphazard.

He looked at us and said, Dad, you're a musician and Mom's a musician." We agreed and he continued, "Well, haven't you had a good life?" We didn't have an answer for that because he knew we had been happy with music. He said, "Well, I'm happy with music. If I can have something like you do I'll be happy."

He enrolled at Pacific Lutheran University (where Dorothy Katherine was teaching) for a year, then transferred to Indiana University and got his bachelor's degree under Joseph Battista, that marvelous teacher and pianist. There he began work on a master's degree.

In his first year of graduate school he had the distinction of playing the Prokofiev *Third Concerto* with the university orchestra. They have a competition each year and choose three soloists. Becky and I drove to Bloomington to hear him one cold, snowy February day. I was proud and happy, and I could see how much happier he was in his chosen field of music than if he had stayed in engineering.

Karl, Joseph Battista, Dorothy, and Becky, 1964

After completing his master's degree at Indiana University in 1965, he married fellow pianist Beverly McGahey and was hired to teach at Morehead State University in Kentucky. He returned to Indiana University for doctoral work in 1969, was divorced, and then married Louise Hanson, a pianist and teacher herself, and they moved to Morehead.

In 1981 they moved to Boulder to study with Guy Duckworth at the University of Colorado, but after a few years they found themselves growing in different directions and agreed to divorce. Karl then decided to leave academe and move to Cincinnati. There he became an independent piano teacher and music director at a large Unity Church, where he played piano and organ and directed three choirs, while also performing regularly at Keyboard Club meetings and recitals. Under his leadership, the Keyboard Club revived its scholarship program for high school students, and started a piano program at the Peaslee Center to provide piano lessons for underserved children and adults. In 1994 he married Susan Rivers Schimpf, enlarging his family by three adult children and four sisters-in-law.

Karl with Revs. Pat and Jack Barker, New Thought Unity Church, 2010

Becky. Becky also majored in piano at Indiana University and studied with Mr. Battista until his untimely death in 1968.

Becky and Dorothy with Mr. and Mrs. Battista, 1966

Sidney Foster kindly took her under his wing to prepare her for her master's recital. He was most helpful and inspiring and helped her through this difficult adjustment. While working on her Master's degree she had an assistantship to teach music theory.

The next year she received a scholarship for study abroad through the Three Arts Club. With her scholarship and a little help from our family fund she went to London for a year, which was a great experience indeed. She studied with Guy Jonson at the Royal Academy of Music and received an L.R.A.M. (Performer's Licentiate of the Royal Academy). She heard much marvelous music and gave a recital at the International Students House. While practicing there for her recital, she met a young man by the name of John Shockley, who was on leave from a graduate program in Political Science at the University of Wisconsin. John had always loved music, and was studying piano in London and practicing on the same piano. They began dating, and soon they had pretty well decided which direction their lives were going.

They returned to the U.S. the next fall and flew to Colorado where John's parents, Martin and Eliza Shockley, have a summer cabin. Becky was as fond of them as they were of her. That fall John returned to Madison, Wisconsin to resume his graduate study while Becky spent the semester in Bloomington. They were married in February of 1970 at a very lovely ceremony in Cincinnati, and they spent most of the next year in Madison.

John's first job was a one-year position at Earlham College in Richmond, Indiana, after which they settled in Macomb, Illinois, where John taught Political Science at Western Illinois University.

Becky gave private lessons there for a while, then entered the doctoral program in piano pedagogy at the University of Colorado at Boulder under Guy Duckworth. After two years in residence she was appointed to the faculty of Eastern Kentucky University in Richmond, where she taught studio and class piano and pedagogy. She gave recitals and workshops, and taught summer piano camps at Kent State University and Eastern Kentucky University.

In 1986 she accepted a position at the University of Minnesota, where she taught pedagogy, class piano, and keyboard skills, and supervised the graduate Piano Teaching Assistants for 28 years. Her research on music learning led to the 1997 publication of her book, Mapping Music, and to lectures for colleges and music teacher organizations in the U.S. and abroad.

Rebecca Shockley, 1998

In 2001, after a long commuter marriage, John retired from Western Illinois University and was hired to teach political science at Augsburg College in Minneapolis. Both are now fully retired and enjoying travel and the rich cultural offerings in the Twin Cities.

PART II: THE KEYBOARD CLUB

The Start of the Club. The Keyboard Club, which grew out of my monthly performances classes for my students, had its first official meeting in September of 1935 at the home of Margaret Welch Tobin, who lived in Northside. At that meeting she was elected president. Since members lived in different parts of the city, it was decided a transportation manager would be needed, and Lucinda Hess was appointed to that task. At that meeting we felt we needed a name for our club. The following were suggested: The Dorothea Music Club, DDD Club, The Keyboard Club, and the Nocturne Music Club. We decided to call it the Keyboard Club, and dues were set at $.75 per year. Little did we know what a long, happy, and fruitful association it would be.

I thought that if a Keyboard Club worked so well for adults why wouldn't it work for students? So that same year we started the Junior Keyboard Club for junior and senior high school students. At our first meeting, Louis Kohnop was elected president. We met at 3 o'clock on Sunday afternoons.

Louis Kohnop, one of her most talented students, made his Cincinnati debut at age 4, performed with the Cincinnati Symphony at age 14, the Chicago Symphony at age 15, and later studied at Juilliard under Olga Samaroff before launching a concert career.

Programs of both Junior and Senior Keyboard Clubs were excellent. Members of the senior club, in addition to playing many solos and two-piano selections, gave interesting papers about various composers and types of music.

In 1937 Keyboard dues were raised to $1.00 per year, and fines were charged for the following:

1. Arriving after 8:15 pm ($.25)
2. Not notifying hostess if one cannot be present ($.50)
3. Not performing on program without a good excuse ($.50)
4. Second offense for no. 3 ($1.00 or performing an entire program later on)

A Concert Featuring Eugene Goossens. On Dec. 8, 1937, the Keyboard Club presented a program of compositions from the works of Eugene Goossens at the Hotel Netherland Plaza. The Keyboarders performed and Mr. Goossens made some remarks, discussing each number before it was performed. The guest artists were Mrs. Oliver Perin, violinist and Mr. Franklin Bens, tenor.

Performing "The Warriors" with Grainger and Goossens. On another occasion, Percy Grainger invited Eugene Goossens and my mother to join him in premiering his six-hand arrangement of "The Warriors," Grainger's "imaginary ballet," in Cincinnati. The original work was commissioned by Sir Thomas Beecham for the Diaghilev Russian Ballet and published in 1926 in two versions - one for three pianos and orchestra and another for two pianos six hands - but was never choreographed. Mother and Goossens rehearsed intensively before Percy arrived in order to achieve the very fast tempos indicated. But when Grainger joined them, he told them it was "much too fast," and when asked about the tempo markings, he replied "Just ignore them." Their performance was the Cincinnati premiere of this work.

Our Monster Concert. By 1939 the Keyboard Clubs were going great. I love experimenting with new ideas, but I guess this time I got a little carried away. I had heard a concert for ten pianos with a conductor, and was fascinated by a whole orchestra of pianists. What an opportunity for all of our Keyboarders.

I thought about this for over a year, and finally approached a student who was a teacher in a local high school. Did she think it possible to secure their nice big stage for such a concert? Her face lit up as she promised to work on this gargantuan undertaking. She found that by combining with the math department, we could give a concert at Walnut Hills High School and split the profits.

A local piano company promised us a room for rehearsal with ten pianos. We ordered music and I worked all summer arranging music, distributing parts, and organizing schedules.

In my home studio on Lorraine Avenue, I worked with groups of two, with two or four watching, then changed performers. My husband drilled groups elsewhere. We had two other pianos moved in temporarily and really slaved over Bach's Prelude from the E Major Violin Partita, *Gitanerias* by Lecuona, *Danse Macabre* by Saint Saëns, and the *Rhapsody in Blue* by Gershwin. Never had we worked so hard as we prepared for our first opportunity to try ten pianos at once six weeks before the concert.

The evening of our first rehearsal came. We were ready for the first number with twenty eager pianists, two at each piano. I raised the baton and off we went on the downbeat.

If I live to be a hundred I never again want to hear such a sound! Our piano store had neglected to have the ten pianos tuned together. E major became a mixture of E flat, D, D flat, etc. Each performer looked at their neighbor accusingly, and I thought my good students had gone berserk. When we discovered the problem, we were reassured as to our musical progress, but discouraged about the situation. Nothing could be done, so that rehearsal was abandoned.

The next day I went to my friends at the Baldwin Piano Company and confided our troubles to them. They had no room with ten pianos tuned alike but would send the necessary ones to the school one week before the concert and we could practice every night. This seemed a very short time to work - and it was. But by superhuman effort we managed to get the program together.

Every night we practiced far into the night. Sometimes the results were bad and sometimes worse, but we persevered. When the night of the dress rehearsal came, some high school boys joined us to work out the lighting effects. As we played the Spanish dance, *Gitanerias*, a red glow, reminiscent of gay bull fights, came over the stage. It was a lovely color, but the pianists raised a cry, "Can't see my music! Can't read a note!" We conferred with the boys, who were unconvinced but agreeable.

Next we played the Bach, which sounded pretty good. But as the ghosts of the *Danse Macabre* crept out of the graves, it was too much for the lighting boys. My students and I suddenly took on an unearthly greenish, ghostly pallor, and the performers cried, "More light, we can't see!" Pandemonium of sound again, and another conference with the student workers about the lights. "But it looks so much like ghosts. Does it really matter if they can't read the music?" pleaded one youngster.

More talk, more music, then our last number, *Rhapsody in Blue*. You guessed it - the temptation was too strong. Halfway through, vivid blue lights appeared, with the same results. (The night of the performance we stationed a teacher by the lighting experts just to be sure no problems arose.)

That night the hall was filled, our pianists performed beautifully with no major catastrophes, and we finished to thunderous applause. We made a little money, as did the math department, and people were at least astonished by the spectacle.

Years later, a well-meaning student said, "Remember our ten piano concert? That was such fun. Why don't we do it again?" I watched the look of horror on my husband's face and replied firmly, "We did it once - but never again!" He had told me immediately following that concert that if we ever tried that again it would be grounds for divorce!

The Keyboard Club Scholarship Fund. I had always been concerned about the difficulty some people have in finding enough money to study. I know I couldn't have made it without a scholarship. Many of our Junior Keyboarders were very good and would like to be able to take advantage of summer programs offered at various universities, but could not afford it. A scholarship fund could be of help to them, so in 1940 the Keyboard Club established a scholarship fund as a memorial to Alma Wuest, a former president, and over the years we found many ways to make that fund grow.

Keyboard Club Special Programs. In addition to our regular monthly meetings we had many special programs. Some of these were just for fun, while others raised money for the scholarship fund. In 1940 we performed a program for the Cincinnati Business Women's Club. In January 1941, we planned an impromptu program. Each member was to be prepared to play something. Each put her name on a slip of paper, which she was asked to fold like a ballot and drop in a basket. When a member's name was drawn she had to play. In February of 1941, two of our Keyboarders gave a program of solo and two-piano music in the Alms Hotel. Admittance was by invitation only. By March 1941, sixty dollars had been set aside for scholarships, and in May, four students entered the competition. The winner was Dorothy Cleaver, then a sophomore at the University of Cincinnati.

The Dorothy Payne Piano Project. *In 1950, Mother started a program to offer free piano lessons to children who could not afford them through the Findlay Street Neighborhood House. Members of the Keyboard Club volunteered to teach the children, and used pianos were donated by the community.*

Two Concerts by Percy Grainger (1948 and 1950)

In February 1948, Percy Grainger came to Cincinnati at the invitation of the Keyboard Club to perform a recital with club members. The program included works for piano solo, two pianos, voice, strings, harp, and reed organ. He stayed in our home, and returned for several subsequent visits. Programs for three Grainger recitals in Cincinnati appear in Appendix II.

In April 1950, he returned with his wife, Ella, to join club members in presenting "An Evening of Chamber Music" at the Cincinnati Art Museum. The program included piano quartets, with Percy Grainger playing along with three Keyboarders, and some works arranged by Grainger for two pianos. There was also a world premier of a Grainger composition for voices, marimbas, and piano. Ella Grainger was the soprano, John Alexander the tenor, and Dewey Owens the baritone. John Alexander also sang some solos Grainger had arranged, and Percy and I played some of his two-piano works. There was also a chorus of Keyboard Club members augmented by several gentlemen.

A unique feature of this concert was the use of four solovoxes, manufactured by Hammond Instruments. These were small organs with about a 2-octave range, which could be placed on a table. Grainger arranged a number of pieces for these instruments, including Bach's A Minor Fugue from WTC Book 1, so that each player could perform one voice of the 4-voice fugue on their instrument. He had always loved the sound of wind instruments, and found these ideally suited to performing polyphonic music.

The Graingers stayed in our home on that occasion, and the four solovoxes were delivered to our house from Hammond Instruments for rehearsals on our dining room table. They were then transported to the Art Museum for the concert.

Photos from Grainger's 1950 Visit

Solovox Rehearsal with three Keyboarders

Dorothy, Percy and Ella

Rehearsal with spinets and solovoxes

Percy and Ella

Percy and four Keyboarders

Percy as flamingo

Two Keyboard Clubs – and a 25th anniversary. In 1954 the Keyboard Club divided into two groups as the membership was increasing. Some wanted meetings in the morning and others in the evening or on Sunday afternoon, so we created a Morning Keyboard and an Afternoon (or Evening) Keyboard.

In 1958, the club held a silver tea at the home of one of the members. After a delightful program presented by the members and a lovely tea prepared by the hostess, everyone dropped money in a basket for our scholarship fund. The tea netted over $200.

Grainger's Last Visit
In March 1958, the club sponsored a recital by Percy Grainger, performing with my mother and other members of the club, at Wilson Auditorium on the University of Cincinnati campus. He arrived several days early to conduct master classes for Keyboarders. The charge was $4 for non-performers and $5 for performers. At the end of the final master class, he performed the Grieg Concerto, with my mother playing the orchestra part on the second piano, and all were visibly moved by the performance. It was his last visit to Cincinnati, as he was quite frail, and he died two years later.

Grainger Recital, 1958

Percy Grainger, 1958

My First Trip to Europe. On April 16, 1958, I left Cincinnati and sailed from New York for that memorable trip to Europe provided by the generosity of the Keyboard Club. I tried to keep the Keyboarders informed as to what I was doing. I arrived home in early June, and gave them a full account of my trip at the Keyboard annual picnic for both groups. I had been able to purchase little mosaic pins in the shape of a violin or mandolin, and gave each Keyboarder one as a token of my appreciation.

After my return we settled down to business as usual. Because we were concerned that our scholarship fund was not growing fast enough, we added $1.00 to the yearly dues.

"Piano Camp" for Keyboarders. In the summer of 1959, after wishing for years that we had time for more quartet playing, a group of Keyboarders organized a musical safari to the cool lakes of northern Michigan. Twenty-four devoted pianists, ranging in age from 40 to 70, set forth on a week of musical labor. It took almost as much planning as the invasion of Normandy. We divided into two groups, staying in the summer homes of two of our members on Lake Charlevoix and Lake Walloon. We met at a third summer home nearby where the large living room accommodated twenty-four ladies and two grand pianos.

Keyboard Campers at Walloon Lake, 1959

Our program seemed to divide itself into three segments each day. We started at 8 a.m. with the first group of sight readers (rotating personnel each day) and worked in hourly sessions. We started with Bach the first day, and each day represented different periods in music history up to the present. Then came a session of the whole group, where we discussed the composer and his contemporaries, some the history of the period, and musical form.

After lunch (which was prepared by a different group each day), we held a technique class for discussing particular problems of playing each composer's music. Then came more sight reading until 6 p.m. when we separated for dinner at any place we chose.

There were a few memorable incidents, such as when one lady, preparing to drive a friend to church, almost backed into the lake amid piercing screams from her companion. Another time a teacher fell down the stairs right into the middle of a horrified technique class, but got up none the worse for wear and proceeded to the problems of Beethoven. It was the first time a teacher had gone on a "sit-down strike" for her students. How well we remember the time one of our fine cooks, who had been hoarding a ham bone and promised bean soup for dinner, got carried away practicing Beethoven and forgot the soup. As we came in the door a large card faced us saying: "Burned the soup. Go out for dinner."

Our Michigan trip was truly marvelous, and in the free hours some members went swimming, while others played more quartets in the homes of local residents. Practice pianos for individuals were also available. For one week secretaries could forget the typewriter, housewives shed family responsibilities and housework, teachers became students, and one lady left her husband for the first time in 45 years. Such is the power of music. One drinks deeply and is everlastingly thirsty for more. We returned home from that exciting summer experience and resumed our monthly meetings in the fall with more enthusiasm than ever.

A Memorable Keyboard Club Concert. Life would be monotonous if everything went according to plan. Monotony was certainly relieved for us at a very special concerto program, which we presented one year at the Alms Auditorium in the Cincinnati Art Museum.

Our four performers had worked long and hard, and we had added a few strings and woodwinds to give orchestral color to the second piano parts. Members and guests totaled about 400, and the auditorium was nearly filled.

All was ready, and the orchestra tuned up on the stage. Our first soloist stepped out amid thunderous applause, ready to play the first movement of Beethoven's *Concerto in c minor*. The second piano and the orchestra played the tutti, and the pianist started on the dynamic first theme with assurance and poise. As always, I breathed a sigh of relief when we really set sail and the concert was under way. On the third page of the piano part we were sailing along when suddenly a loud crash interrupted the music. I glanced around. All the players looked okay but a bit bewildered. Then I looked in the direction of the pianist and realized the pedals had fallen off!

After bravely continuing for a short time, the pianist turned to the audience and said in a very composed voice, "I'm sorry, but I can't continue without the pedals."

What to do? Suddenly the stage was filled with helpers from the audience. The violinists and cellists were crawling under the piano, and everyone had an idea, but we couldn't get the pedals to stay in place.

Then some bright soul suggested placing books in back of the pedal stand and to each side to hold them in place after the metal rods were inserted. The museum guards finally produced some books that were not museum pieces, and with the help of dozens of willing workers, the pedals stayed in place. Wobbly they were, but they worked.

Order was restored and the music of Mr. Beethoven was again the center of interest. The performer still insists that she never played as well before or since. She explained, "The pedals fell off but that wasn't my fault, so I just relaxed and enjoyed playing." The other performers seemed equally relaxed, and it was a memorable evening in many ways.

A Halloween Party and Other Oddities. I've been talking about the Keyboard Club's special programs, but through the years we've had a lot of fun at regular meetings, particularly when special events have been planned. For one meeting we held a Halloween party, for which every performer was to come masked and wearing a costume depicting her piece. What a strange group we were and what a hilarious evening we had.

When one figure, garbed in a fisherman's hat and long raincoat, went to the piano and started to play, we immediately guessed Chopin's *Raindrop Prelude*. We guessed the performer by the way her little fingers turned in.

Then came a tall lady in a witch's costume with a plump partner in short pants, shirt and tousled wig. What else but the *Sorcerer's Apprentice* of Dukas, played as a duet.

One weird looking character came out in a paper dry cleaning bag, with holes cut out for eyes, nose, and mouth, and played the old fashioned *Sack Waltz* - not highbrow, but fun. Another lovely Spanish lady wearing a beautiful black lace mantilla went on to play the *Spanish Caprice* of Moszkowski. She had not memorized it, so she started playing brilliantly and confidently with her music. On the third page she faltered as her mask slipped over her eyes. It had been jarred loose by the energy of her playing. From then on it was a fight to the finish: Play - Adjust mask - Play - Adjust mask - etc. She stayed with it until the bitter end and won a hearty round of applause for her performance. Among other qualities, music performance develops quick thinking in emergencies as well as dogged determination.

Those Keyboarders! Strange things happen to them whether they are at a party or performing in a concert, or even just by themselves. One lady who had resumed piano study after having raised five children was terribly nervous on the occasion of her first performance in one of Keyboard's practice classes. She arose very early in order to practice for her debut. She hurried to take her shower, turned on the water, and discovered she was fully attired in her pajamas, which by this time were dripping wet. Well, people say that musicians are crazy...!

The Keyboard Club's European Trip. After the Keyboarders returned from that delightful vacation in Michigan, we spent quite a bit of time talking about composers and their homes, and somehow an idea started to circulate among the group: If Keyboarders could travel to Michigan, why couldn't they travel to Europe and visit these musical shrines?

Finally, late in 1961, we consulted a travel agent. One student who had traveled extensively with her husband laid the groundwork and we met with the agent to discuss our ideas. Fortunately she was patient and hard working and made some sense out of our ideas.

We wanted to take in the Lucerne, Salzburg, and Edinburgh festivals. We had to visit the museums of Beethoven, Schubert, and Mozart at their birthplaces. We didn't want to go to a different city each day, but spend two to four days in the most interesting places. We didn't want to be part of a big group but travel on our own. We needed a guide. We wanted to take in any places of musical interest along the way. We wanted good hotels, but not luxury ones. It was a big order, but by contacting a Swiss travel agency and working some minor miracles she was able to arrange a trip for us.

In July 1962, our group of ten got under way. There were seven middle aged women and three teenagers, including my daughter Becky, along with Susie and Tally, two of her Junior Keyboard buddies. Four flew to Italy first, as that wasn't on our itinerary. The rest of us sailed on the *United States*.

We arrived in London and immediately loved this bustling, historic and magnificent city. All the streets, monuments, palaces, and buildings that we had read about suddenly came to life. We found the English people friendly, helpful, and interested in our tour. But we were utterly defeated by their monetary system, so when it came time to tip, we simply held out a handful of coins and said to the waitress, "Take some."

There had been no advance notice of summer concerts, but upon arrival we found a "London Festival" in progress. So, between Madame Tussaud's Wax Museum and the changing of the guard at Buckingham Palace, we heard Handel's *Jeptha* at the Guildhall, a 15th century building in the City of London. None of our group knew the opera, but we were really thrilled by it. Hearing Handel's great music in the Guildhall with strings and harpsichord was truly an experience we shall remember. The chorus, robed and standing on each side of the stage and not participating in the dramatic scenes, was most impressive.

This performance had great significance because Handel had lived in London for many years. Later we visited Westminster Abbey and felt we were on hallowed ground when we saw the place where Handel is buried. We were told that he was the only foreigner to be so honored by the English. It seemed so fitting to find artists, poets, writers, and musicians buried with royalty in this historic old abbey. Often they were not appreciated during their lives, so at least after death they were finally given some of the honor due them.

Our group, all being musicians, had a common bond which made this trip such a success. When our friends from Italy arrived and met us in Paris, we started on our trip in a little blue bus driven by a pleasant Swiss-Frenchman named Charlie. Our guide was an American pianist, Martha, who was studying with Alfred Cortot in Paris. Charlie spoke no English, but after a few days of driving our jolly group, he told Martha he wished he understood what we said because we laughed so much he must be missing a lot. He also smiled as we sang along the way and wished he could join in. During the tour he learned to say "Good Morning," "Good Night," "Thank you," and "See you later." We reciprocated with rather limited vocabulary of "Bonjour," "Merci," "Bonne nuit," and "Dormez bien."

When we were in Germany and had acquired a few phrases, one of our more elegant ladies descended from the bus after a concert and said to Charlie in her most charming manner, "Grüss Gott and Bonsoir, Charlie." He smiled but looked a little confused.

In Paris there were no concerts - only a performance at the opera which was sold out. However, we discovered to our great joy that at the Bibliothèque Nationale there was a special exhibit of Debussy letters, manuscripts, and pictures commemorating the hundredth anniversary of his birth. What a thrill to be in a large room with fascinating mementos of a musical genius. There were sketches of costumes and settings for *Afternoon of a Faun* and *Pelléas and Mélisande*, as well as original manuscripts of piano, voice, and symphonic works.

We felt we saw the human side of a great composer: pictures taken with musical friends on happy occasions, and serious photographs of this great Frenchman with the penetrating and dreamy eyes. These personal things make a composer come alive. He lived, loved, composed, studied, performed, agonized over his writings, was hungry and poor many times, unhappy and rebellious most of the time, but this human being left a legacy of beauty and ethereal loveliness to the world that will never be lost. Of course Paris was exciting, lovely and fun, but for us the highlight was our visit to the Debussy exhibit.

Later we passed a building with a simple plaque, which said in French, "In this building Frederic Chopin died." Here we were walking the same streets where Chopin had lived and died.

In Germany we travelled to Koblenz, then to Bonn, where we made a pilgrimage to the Beethoven museum and saw some facsimiles of his great works, including the Moonlight Sonata. After a fire in the museum several years before, set by a mentally disturbed person, his desk, piano, and some manuscripts had been destroyed. We were touched to see his tragic death mask, pathetic ear trumpets, each one larger than the last but always ineffective, pictures, programs, letters, instruments, and manuscripts showing the agony of creation.

After being in a composer's home and seeing the small barren room where he was born, we got a feeling of being close to him. It reminded us that where one is born is less important than what one contributes to life. Beethoven's great outpouring of emotion, intensity, anger, frustration, love, sympathy, and above all, beauty surely attests to this. No problems of life could stop that God-given talent from expressing itself.

From Bonn, the trip up the Rhine on a steamer was delightful. We enjoyed the busy life of the river with its boat traffic as we went past towering cliffs, medieval fortresses and castles, including the Stolzenfels Castle, supposedly built by a branch of the Stolzenbach family many years ago.

In Germany we ate good hearty food, and we enjoyed the singing that seems to be part of their way of life.

We stopped in Wiesbaden, a beautiful city. Our old fashioned hotel was immaculate and spoke of past glories. We strolled through the city and visited a fine music store where we bought some Peters editions of music quite inexpensively. That evening we went to a concert in the park where the orchestra was really bad. They played a Gluck overture and everyone played in a different key. For the next number the ones who had played it one way decided to adopt the other and visa versa. It was really hilarious. The *Vienna Woods* sounded as German as sausage and had none of the light hearted gaiety of the Viennese. But we did enjoy the elderly German couples so neatly dressed, smiling, and just enjoying the music in a non-critical way.

We went to Heidelberg with its great university, founded in 1386. We went to an interesting old restaurant where the walls were covered with names and dates chalked there through the years. After a lunch of venison and red cabbage, Becky got into the spirit of the place and wrote, "Keyboard Club, Cincinnati, Ohio." So now we are immortalized on the wall of that restaurant.

We visited Baden-Baden, the magnificent Black Forest, passed Lake Constance, and went on to Bregenz, Austria, where we saw an operetta performed on a boat in the lake. Many people were in attendance for the spectacle of lights, carts, masks, and finally fireworks, all mixed with rather mediocre music, but it was unusual and the location was most picturesque.

After traveling for some time, we came to Munich and stayed at the Schottenhamel Hotel where Dorothy and I had stayed in 1958. It was very comfortable and homey, and in the dining room there were canaries at each window, with an orchestra playing lovely music. We were there on my wedding anniversary, August 1, so at dinner some of our group told the orchestra conductor that it was my anniversary and asked him to play a proper song. They presented us with a delicious chocolate torte, just as the orchestra began playing "Happy Birthday." We sang and smiled back at the beaming maestro. The good wishes were there, and the song didn't really matter. After dinner we went to a marionette performance of *Die Kluge* by Carl Orff. It was extraordinary, as the recording was excellent and the marionettes seemed so real. We enjoyed the music and the performance a lot.

Munich, rebuilt after the war, was an interesting combination of old castles, such as the Nymphenburg Palace, birthplace of King Ludwig II, and modern apartments, churches and stores. We went on to Vienna, that musical city, where the war had taken a terrible toll and many buildings had been destroyed, but the spirit of the Viennese could not be downed.

Our guide told us a wonderful anecdote that came out of the Russian occupation. It seems that while the Russians were in Austria they sent out notices that there would be a great May Day parade. They would have many Communist troops and many festivities, and a big long parade that would last for hours in downtown Vienna. Since the Viennese were not the rulers, they had nothing to say about it, but they devised their own scheme to upset the plans. On the day of the great parade, all the stores were open, trams were running, taxicabs ran, and no streets were blocked off to traffic. There was one tremendous traffic jam as the parade tried to get through. Every street was clogged with people because everyone had come to town. After struggling for an hour to get through the masses, which they could not disperse, the Communists gave up the parade. That was one way of resisting the occupation, and they certainly did not appreciate the Russians.

One of the very beautiful little towns we visited in Austria after leaving Vienna was Gemunden. It was on a lake surrounded by beautiful mountains, so we stopped there for lunch and were told that there was a Brahms museum in the town. Our guide tried to find out where it was, but there seemed to be great confusion about it since it was across a bridge they were building and in a part of the town that was still in a state of disrepair.

Some of us stout-hearted people went to where we thought it should be, at least where we had been told it was, and started up the stairs. We were met by a very sour-faced lady with a huge ring of keys who was muttering something in German. Several of our group knew enough German to understand that she was telling us the museum was closed and we couldn't go in. Another member tried to tell her that we had come all the way from the United States and were very interested in this museum, but she sternly shook her head and refused to let us in.

About this time a man who lived in the building came by. He spoke some English and seemed to sense the difficulty when we explained, so he said to the lady, "These people must go in to see the museum. They've come a long way and you can let them in. I'll stay with them. It will be all right, I promise you." At first she was reluctant, but he was very persuasive. Finally she unlocked the door and we went in. We figured that the reason she was so reluctant for us to come in was that it was in a bad state of repair. It was dirty and messy and looked like it hadn't been dusted for ages. But inside we found beautiful pictures of Brahms and some pictures of his friends. There was, what I guess to be, his famous umbrella, but of course we don't know whether or not it was really his. The house had not been lived in since it had been made into a museum. When we looked out the window we got a beautiful view of the lake and mountains, and in the center of the living room was Brahms' piano. It was old but it looked like a very lovely piano. One of the ladies had the temerity to ask the guide, "Can our teacher play something on that?" I said, "Oh no, you can never touch pianos in museums." Our friend looked around and said, "There's nothing that says you can't, so go ahead." So I sat down and played Brahms' *Scotch Intermezzo* on Brahms' own piano. I was thrilled, as were all our Keyboarders, and several of them took pictures. (It was a little dark, so just one of them turned out.) As we went back to our bus we didn't say anything, but we thought about what an experience it was to have been in the very house where Brahms had stayed, to have played on his piano, and to have seen so many things that reminded us of him.

After Gemunden we moved on to Salzburg, where we stayed in the Hotel Pechert, the same one where Dorothy Katherine and I had stayed. All the ladies in the group loved Salzburg on sight. It is a lovely town and some of it is much as it was in Mozart's time. There are mountains all around and a fortress on the hill. We were thankful we could be in the town where Mozart lived and worked and produced so many of his great compositions.

The first night we were there we had tickets for a marionette performance of *Bastien und Bastienne*, an opera Mozart composed when he was 12 years old. The story tells of shepherds and shepherdesses who test each other's love through so-called sorcery until the sorcerer finally draws them together. At first the figures seemed very small, but as the opera continued, it seemed so real that the characters seemed to come alive. It was beautifully done, with a wonderful recording. They also did a puppet show of *Eine Kleine Nachtmusik*. For that I didn't feel like I needed the puppets, since I can just listen to that music and enjoy it. Next they did a beautiful performance of the *Nutcracker Suite*. Everyone in our group felt so good about being in this wonderful place.

The next morning we set out to hear Mozart's great *C minor Mass* at St. Peter's Cathedral, where it was first performed. Our guide had secured tickets for us, and the enormous cathedral was filled. In fact, we looked in the back and saw many people who stood for the entire performance, listening quietly and reverently to the music. The orchestra, organ, and chorus were at the back of the cathedral. The voices were lovely and there was nothing to distract us from listening. We were struck by the fact that this is where Mozart conducted it, and this is where it first began. And we think how dramatic and how moving it is today. It is so full of faith and conviction. The *Credo* and the *Gloria* brought tears to our eyes. It lasted well over an hour, but no one moved. People who think that Mozart is always light and gay should hear this great work.

In the afternoon we went sightseeing with a local guide who was full of authority. When we got out of our bus to go somewhere, she would stand in the middle of the rather crowded street and hold up her hand in the best policeman's tradition, stopping traffic so we could cross the street. She looked charming in her Austrian dirndl and took us about so briskly that we covered lots of ground.

The Mirabelle Palace had been the archbishop's residence when Salzburg was a separate province, and the gardens were lovely. Much of the furniture had been removed during the war. We also saw the very famous Keller's Hotel. The fortress on the hill, dating back to the 11th century, was most impressive, with its hiding places in the stone catacombs for Christians fleeing persecution. We saw an ancient burial ground at the foot of the steps leading up to the fortress, and realized that this was where Mozart's sister and Haydn's brother are buried.

We passed the old riding academy, a bakery that had been in the same place for 400 years, more cathedrals, and then went on to Mozart's birthplace. On the first floor was a very interesting display of scenes from Mozart's operas, and on other floors were other famous, fascinating mementos of his life. The well-known painting of himself, his sister, and his father, as well as a painting of his mother, were placed near the piano and the harpsichord. We later attended a concert at the Mozart Town House, near the Hotel Bristol. The Mozarts lived here when they were more prosperous and had moved across the Salz River from the older section of Salzburg to the newer. Here their music room was large enough to seat 80 and had been restored after some destruction from World War II. Now it is a lovely room with famous paintings and glass cases containing some of the instruments Mozart had used in his day, such as the cello, violin, viola, etc. We heard a concert there in which they performed some Mozart songs and two violin and piano sonatas with a piano that is a reproduction of his piano. It had a lovely, light tone, very suitable for chamber music. In the evening we heard an orchestral concert at the Mozarteum, a conservatory named in honor of Mozart, where a great many Americans go to study. We hated to leave all the lovely memories of Mozart in Salzburg, but we all hoped to come back someday, and now it was time to move on.

We went from there to the Lucerne Festival in Switzerland. Lucerne is a charming city, so clean and colorful. The world-famous covered bridge dates back hundreds of years, with pictures of life in Lucerne in the old days painted on the inside walls.

After checking into our hotel, we were met by my former student and dear friend, Millie Schmidt, who had lived in Cincinnati for ten years and knew many of the Keyboarders. It was a happy reunion for all of us. That evening we went to our first concert in the beautiful festival hall, which is very spacious with many fountains in front. The acoustics inside were excellent. We heard the Berlin Philharmonic play the *Egmont Overture* and Mozart's *G minor Symphony*, followed by a concert version of Bartok's *Bluebeard's Castle*. I wondered what would happen, because at some other concerts with unfamiliar strange modern music, there had been much muttering among the Keyboarders. I remember that the younger members of the group had liked them, but the older members were not as receptive to such sounds. They practically sat on their hands and did not applaud.

I found this concert version absolutely spine chilling. It was so dramatic, so well done, and even though we knew how it was going to end, we kept thinking that the last wife believed that Bluebeard loved her and that she loved him. Surely she can stop him from this act, which is about to happen, I thought, as the tension grew. I noticed that Becky and I were clasping our hands together, and I think the two other young girls were sitting on the edge of their seats. At the moment when the wife finally screamed, realizing she was to be killed, we almost jumped out of our seats. I shall always remember that Tally's mother did not appreciate it. (She turned to her daughter when it was over and said, "You don't dare applaud.") But almost everyone else applauded.

On another night we heard Elisabeth Schwarzkopf in the *Four Last Songs* of Strauss, followed by Beethoven's *Symphony No. 8* and Bartok's *Concerto for Orchestra*. Every night was filled with delightful and inspiring music.

One of the highlights of our visit to Lucerne was a master class by the famous Hungarian pianist, Géza Anda. He is such a fine pianist, whom we all admired. Our Swiss friend Millie had written ahead and asked if we could, for a fee, audit the class for one afternoon, and we were permitted to do so.

We went up, up, and up a high hill to reach the Conservatory. It was a beautiful old building and the lady who was in charge greeted us very graciously. We waited for Mr. Anda to arrive. As he strode in briskly, the directress went up to him and explained that we were the group from America who wanted to audit the class. He turned and shook hands with all of us and welcomed us warmly. Then we all went upstairs to where the class was to be held. This class started at 2 p.m. and we had to leave at 6 p.m. because we were going to another concert, but they were still going strong when we left. We went downstairs and asked the directress what fee we should pay. She answered, "None. Mr. Anda said you were to be his guests." We all profited from his class.

We talked afterwards about the class and how interesting it was. We were all impressed with Mr. Anda's linguistic ability. When English or American students played he went into their language very easily. If it was a German student he spoke German just as fluently, and when a French girl played he was equally at home in French. This made it so easy for all the participants. We didn't always understand the German or parts of the French, but we always understood when he demonstrated things he wanted corrected. We found one of his phrases particularly amusing. There was a very good English pianist who played a Beethoven sonata. Though she played technically very well, she had a tendency to over pedal. His first comment on the Beethoven was, "It has too much gravy." That phrase always comes to my mind when I hear a pianist using too much pedal.

It was time to leave Lucerne, but before we left we visited one of the homes of Richard Wagner, a lovely villa high on a hill overlooking Lake Lucerne and now a museum. There we saw many pictures, his piano, his famous velvet jacket, his velvet beret, and the pictures of his wedding to Franz Liszt's daughter, Cosima, which took place in the villa. It made us feel very close to the great composer.

The guide told one anecdote that we particularly enjoyed. She said the previous owners of the villa had invited Wagner to visit. They admired him greatly, and he was very happy there as he could compose in peace amid beautiful surroundings. He was so pleased that he decided to stay, so they moved out and left the villa to him for as long as he chose. He stayed about seven years! (He surely stayed a good bit longer than the man who came to dinner!)

From Lucerne we went to Zurich and had a lovely lunch before boarding our plane for Edinburgh, where we were to attend the last big festival of our trip in Europe. We were all looking forward to it, as it is one of the most famous festivals in the world.

We settled into our hotel in Edinburgh. It was a small, comfortable hotel converted from a rather large home. We were amused to discover that the room adjoining ours had been converted into a bathroom – a very spacious bathroom with a fireplace in it! (This was my first experience with a fireplace in the bathroom!)

The food was good and the help very nice, and we liked the Scottish people immediately. They were warm and friendly and somewhat different from the English, but in other ways a great deal the same.

The city itself is fascinating, with its gray buildings and many chimney pots which can be seen everywhere. It was almost untouched by the war. High on a hill is a huge fortress, which has overlooked the entire city for centuries. When we went up there we found it to be one of the most interesting places we had seen. We particularly liked a small chapel that one of the queens had used. It is part of the National Trust and is kept in a good state of repair.

The opening night of the festival begins with a traditional military tattoo. One member of our group had been there before and talked a lot about it. It didn't mean much to us, but we knew that since it was opening night we wanted to see it. It was a very cold night in August, and we almost felt as if we were going to a football game as we climbed into the bleachers overlooking the grounds. We had taken some blankets with us and were happy to have them.

When the floodlights shone down onto this enormous courtyard and the bagpipers started their march onto the field, it was a thrilling spectacle. There were hundreds of kilts of various tartans representing the different Scottish clans. That sight, together with the sound of all those bagpipes in the great outdoors, made it the most thrilling outdoor concert I have ever heard. Then came the various bands of the royal navy and the royal army. There were Indian horsemen with their turbans and representatives from all the British colonies - Irish, Canadian, etc. This enormous parade passed with bagpipe music much of the time and music of the official military bands at other times.

At one point in the intermission they welcomed certain groups to the festival. As we were listening to the names of the dignitaries and special groups, we heard over the loudspeaker, "We are glad to welcome members of the Keyboard Club from Cincinnati, Ohio." We looked at each other in disbelief and clapped just as loudly for ourselves as for the others. We didn't know how this came about unless our guide had spoken to someone in charge.

As we left the grounds, we decided we weren't very far from our hotel and perhaps could walk, or at least walk over to Princess St. and find our way. By the time we got to Princess St. we were so cold that our teeth started to chatter. We spied a chocolate shop and the three young girls said, "Let's go in." It was a perfectly charming little place that served no coffee, no tea, only hot chocolate. Nothing ever tasted quite so good. When we came out onto the street we realized we were farther from our hotel than we thought. We decided to take a bus, but which bus? We didn't know. We only knew where our hotel was but we didn't know how far. As we stood in the queue, which is the usual way to wait for a bus in Scotland and England, we asked a Scottish lady if she could tell us which bus to take and where to get off. She tried to explain, but I think she thought we looked rather uncertain. She stopped the bus for us and said, "I'll show you; follow me." She shepherded us into the bus and told the bus driver where we wanted to get off, then, waving gaily to us, she got off. Everything about Edinburgh is charming and old world, and we loved Princess Street with its modern shops, including china shops and tartan shops. Walking at night under the yellow streetlights that made us look like ghouls, we loved the eerie atmosphere they created. We also enjoyed visiting Holyrood Castle, which is beautiful and historic.

The next morning we went to a concert of chamber music featuring a Brahms quintet and a Shostakovich quartet. After our experience in Lucerne where some of the ladies were audibly unhappy with Bartok, I wondered how they would react to Shostakovich, but in we went and sat down in the third row. Of course the Brahms was a joy and everybody loved it. Such beautiful music, and beautifully played. Then came the Shostakovich, which turned out to be quite accessible. I didn't find it as far out as the Bartok, even though it was composed more recently. I kept glancing at my friends, and even among the older members I saw nobody looking unhappy or muttering - for which I was grateful. I was beginning to think they were starting to absorb some of this type of music. Of course our three young members ate it up as they did all the modern things, since they were young in heart and spirit.

When the quartet finished, they stood up to take their bows and everybody clapped loud and long. Suddenly the first violinist pointed his bow in our direction. I was afraid we had done something wrong. As heads turned toward us, we looked around, and in the row directly behind us sat Dmitri Shostakovich. He had been sitting behind us the whole time. I don't know how much English he knew, but fortunately no one had complained. He went up onstage and took his bows very modestly, looking as if he would have preferred being any other place than where he was. When he came back to his seat we asked if we could have his autograph on our programs. He very graciously signed every one of our programs. That program is one of my treasured possessions. Since he rarely comes to our country and doesn't play too many times in Europe, it was great to see him and to notice how modest in appearance he was.

What a little man, but what great musical ideas! I have always enjoyed his music, and since that time a number of our Keyboarders have studied his preludes and some of his chamber works. I think they are beginning to understand him now.

The next night we heard a big orchestral concert at the large concert hall in Edinburgh. There we heard Shostakovich's Cello Concerto performed by the great Rostropovich. I had never heard of this cellist before, and neither had anyone in our group. The effect was magical - such a beautiful tone, such musicianship, such authority, and such everything! He is truly a great artist. At that time he was well known in Europe but hadn't played much in the United States. But now he is well known here, and whenever he performs here the tickets are immediately sold out. Shostakovich was also there that night.

The next day we spent sightseeing. The guides were charming and friendly and called us "Darling." We all loved Edinburgh and with reluctance took the night train to London. The train was very comfortable, and in the morning we were awakened by a knock at the door. The steward asked if we wanted tea. This was very nice, since we arrived in London too early to get breakfast on the train. I like the British custom of having tea. No matter where you are, aboard ship or on a train or any place at all, taking tea is the custom.

We had just a few days in London, that lovely city, before taking the boat train for Southampton in order to board the *America* for our homeward journey (This was nearly the last voyage made by that boat.)

We boarded in the evening, had a nice dinner, and settled cozily into our cabins. Sometime early in the morning the steward came and closed our portholes. I wondered what was wrong, but before morning we knew. We were in the midst of a rather vicious hurricane. The ship went from side to side and up and down, and most of our group were seasick. I thought I had the strongest stomach in the world and that a rough sea would never affect me, but believe me it did.

We were told to go up on deck as we might feel better there. I went, but I certainly didn't feel better, and neither did some of the others. I stayed in my cabin most of the time, but the young ones in our group and a few of the ladies braved the dining room.

The storm was at its height the night of the Captain's Dinner when everybody puts on a fancy little hat and pretends to be very happy. There weren't many in the dining room, but they snapped photos just the same. One of our very elegant ladies with her little paper hat was just beginning to feel the effects of the weather when the photographer took her picture. You've never seen a more forlorn face with a paper hat on her head. We've all saved that picture and it is one of our treasured possessions.

One of our young members went up on the deck then came down just as I did. As I was lying on the bed she came in looking very pale. I asked her, "Are you sick? Do you think you'd feel better down here?" She said, "I don't know. I only want to be close to my life preserver."

This went on for three days. It was a vicious storm. When we felt better we went up on deck to see the tremendous waves. Some of the sailors told us that this really wasn't so bad; sometimes the waves go over the top deck. In fact, one sailor had been swept overboard in one of these gales. Maybe it could have been worse, but I hope I never see it.

The day before we came into New York harbor, the storm abated and we had a beautiful day, but we were a bedraggled looking group of Keyboarders.

After we arrived home we could hardly wait to tell the other members all about our experiences in Europe. We resumed our regular meetings, more eager than ever to perform the compositions of the composers with whom we had become better acquainted.

House Tours. We still wanted to raise more money for the scholarship fund. We felt that more of our very talented students who had worked so hard preparing for the auditions should have opportunities to attend some of the excellent summer programs offered at various universities. Then we came up with an idea. House tours were very much in vogue. A number of our members had lovely homes in Cincinnati's better suburbs. Why not try a musical house tour? We could sell tickets for people to visit these beautiful homes where they could pause for a while and enjoy some lovely piano music.

In 1965, members from both junior and senior groups, along with younger students of Keyboard Club teachers, prepared pieces to perform on the tour. Each was assigned to be at a certain house for a specified interval so that there would be continuous music at each home. We worked long and hard, and it was a great success! So successful, in fact, that we repeated the project the following year, with equally successful results.

Vronsky and Babin Concert and Master Classes. In 1969 we sponsored a concert by the well-known two-piano team of Vronsky and Babin, whom I had first met in Aspen. The concert took place in Eden Park at the Playhouse In The Park. This concert was also a great success, and our scholarship fund grew even more. In fact, the fund was getting so large that our treasurers didn't really like the idea of handling all that money. So after the concert we turned the money over to the Greater Cincinnati Foundation, which manages such funds for various organizations throughout the city. The fund was named The Dorothy S. Payne Scholarship Fund, and it was certainly one of my most cherished dreams come true.

Vronsky and Babin

The Babins gave several master classes when they were here. Victor Babin was a commanding teacher and had such a marvelous personality that students responded very well. Their fright was forgotten when they started to play and when he worked with them. They were so intent on doing what he wanted that they forgot to be scared. I imagine that for the rest of their lives they will always remember the comments he made to them and how inspirational he was, along with Vitya's interesting sidelights. As a result of this experience, some of the students later went on to summer study at the Cleveland Institute of Music where the Babins were teaching. The students were most inspired there as well.

The Payne Family Concerts. In 1974 the four of us were invited by the Keyboard Club to present a Payne Family Concert. Indian Hill High School has a large, beautiful auditorium, so it was chosen as the site for the concert. After consulting family members as to their availability when the auditorium would be free, they set the date for November 30th. We conferred with each other by phone and by mail as to what we should play. We planned some numbers for two pianos/eight hands, some for two pianos/four hands, and some solos. We made sure each person had his own part to practice at home, as we actually had only a couple of days to rehearse together. The committee worked very hard decorating, selling tickets, and taking care of all the details.

The day arrived snowy and blustery, and we wondered if anyone would come out on such an evening. Then people started coming, and they came and they came, till the auditorium was almost full. Even though

1st Payne Family Recital, 1974

the roads were slick and driving was quite treacherous, the bad weather had not deterred our audience. The Keyboard Club sold recordings of the concert, and the proceeds were all turned over to the Scholarship Fund. What a joy to be able to perform

2nd Payne Family Recital, 1979

with my own children and thereby add a considerable sum to my pet project, the Scholarship Fund.

The Keyboarders were so pleased with the first Payne Family Concert that they asked if we would do another, which we did in 1979. To be safe from snowy, blustery weather, we chose a date in May, and even more tickets were sold for this concert, which further enriched our scholarship fund. Junior Keyboarders served as ushers, and the stage was decorated with spring flowers. The concert went very well and, as before, a delightful reception was held for us after the program.

In between the two concerts, in 1975, we celebrated the 40th anniversary of the Keyboard Club with a special dinner at the Kenwood Country Club.

Recitals, Workshops, and Meetings. The Keyboard Club continued to sponsor recitals, usually at the Taft Museum, as well as workshops and master classes led by visiting artists and professors. In 1984, Professor Guy Duckworth from the University of Colorado at Boulder, gave group master classes for members.

Although Victor Babin passed away in 1972, his widow, Vitya Vronsky, continued to visit periodically from Cleveland to conduct very fine classes for Keyboarders and others who wished to attend.

In 1990, Karl. Jr. was invited to perform Victor Babin's 2-piano arrangements of J. S. Bach's six Trio Sonatas with Vitya Vronsky in a concert at the Cleveland Institute of Music. It was a thrilling experience for him, and he has a recording of that concert.

Most importantly, the Keyboard Club, after many years, continues its monthly meetings where members can play for each other and socialize a bit.

Over the years the membership has changed as new people begin to study and former members leave for one reason or another, but many who move out of town still try to keep in touch. Working together with music provides a bond of friendship unlike anything else.

PART III: REFLECTIONS ON MUSIC AND PIANO TEACHING

In this section, I should like to discuss my thoughts and observations about music in general, and piano teaching in particular. When one pursues the same occupation for many years, one is bound to make many observations and develop certain ideas on the subject. So it has been with me. Teaching piano has been more than an occupation. For our entire family, "piano" has been a way of life. We feel that each house from the most humble dwelling to the largest mansion - must have a piano in order for that house to be a home.

When our eldest daughter Dorothy Katherine was two and a half years old we visited a favorite aunt during the Christmas holidays. After an interesting train ride, we journeyed to her lovely apartment where there was a trimmed tree, presents waiting and aromas of good things cooking. Our daughter took all of this in with eyes aglow, exclamations, and joy. Suddenly she stood stark still, surveyed the living room and asked soberly, "Aunt Margie, where is your 'plando'?" When Aunt Margie admitted she didn't have a piano, Dorothy Katherine looked at her with a puzzled expression. She whimpered sadly, "Poor Aunt Margie, no 'plando'."

As our family grew so did our instrument collection. In our home it was not a car for each adult, but a piano (at least one!) for every member of the family - a very musical quintet. At one time our instrument collection included seven pianos, an old harmonium, assorted violins, two guitars, a mandolin, bongos, a clarinet, a saxophone, and a harpsichord. It's a wonderful life to live in a family of musicians and be able to associate with students and friends who love music with an overwhelming passion.

One adult student said to me after a year's study, "I thought I'd like to take a few piano lessons for fun. Look at me. I practice like mad; my three children all study and practice almost as much; and most remarkable of all, my husband comes home from his office and practices five-finger studies so he won't be left out of the new way of life. We remodeled the living room to make room for a new grand piano, and we drive our old car to pay for this expense. It's even more amazing that I love every minute of it and hope I live long enough to play really well."

Music is like that - all absorbing, and like true faith, our love of music can become an impregnable fortress, a veritable tower of strength against every vicissitude that may assail us in moments of chaos, travail, and illness. Music can also help us to express the joy and thankfulness we feel within.

Chopin wrote some of his loveliest nocturnes and polonaises as he waged a losing battle against the ravages of tuberculosis. Exiled from Russia at 44 by internal revolts, Rachmaninoff fled to America where he became a still greater composer and the greatest pianist of his day. Mozart's married life was one of domestic strife, loss of young children, and abject poverty that followed him even to his grave, yet in his short life span of 36 years, he wrote some of the loveliest music our ears have ever heard. Bach buried 11 of his 20 children in infancy yet proceeded to compose great and profound music, all the while praising God for His goodness and mercy. Bach's divine genius at counterpoint assuaged a grief that would otherwise have been unbearable.

We could go on and on, but what everyone must realize is that every life has its joys and sorrows, and studying and performing great music can be a source of strength and comfort. Worries, burdens, self-pity, and forebodings cannot

survive a practice session, for example, on Beethoven's Moonlight Sonata, whether for the faltering amateur or the self assured professional. It requires every bit of one's mental powers, physical exertion, and great concentration. After an hour or more of intense work, one leaves the piano uplifted and refreshed. I'm sure the same benefits can be derived from any other musical practice, but my experience has been largely with piano, so to that field I shall confine my thoughts.
To sum it up, if there is a piano in the house, and if it is used, life is likely to be more interesting, exciting and rewarding.

The Musical Amateurs - God Bless Them. In our world today, as never before, we need specialists. We have them in medicine, science, education, drama, painting, and all facets of life where progress is paramount. The world also needs specialists in music, professional musicians. They learn all about music performing, composing, and conducting.
In the United States today, there are many fine schools of music turning out well-trained musicians each year. As one artist aptly put it, "Musicians no longer need to go to Europe to study. Our American schools have become equal or better than many of the great European schools."

Our professional American musicians are constantly improving, but far too many aspire only to careers of performing, conducting, or composing. Too often, as a last resort, they turn to teaching music and hope to teach little Mozarts.

What about the thousands of eager amateurs? They are a challenge to a teacher, especially adult students who study music for the sheer joy of playing great music. Timid and self-conscious, with no aspirations to startle the world, they often have to be cajoled into performing for friends and family. But I find this type of student most rewarding to work with.

Housewives, businessmen and women, teachers, doctors, secretaries, and people from all walks of life, can share their love of music as a common bond.

Playing music for oneself is fine, but sharing music with others is more exciting. The aim of the Keyboard Club is to get students to know more about music through study and performance. How exciting to have worked on the Chopin *A-flat Polonaise*, trying to interpret it properly, memorizing it, and finally, with trembling fingers, actually play it for a meeting of fellow students. At the end, resounding applause, exclamations such as, "That really was great!" " How you have improved since the last time." "Such strength! What have you been doing?" and even the ultimate, "I heard it at a concert last week and you do it just as well."

Degrees of difference in all endeavors are striking. Some people do have more intelligence, talent, or personality. The musical amateur must realize early that devoting one or two hours a day to piano practice will not make his playing sound like Claudio Arrau's. But he can play well, give great pleasure to himself and his friends, promote the cause of good music, and best of all, become an intelligent listener.

Nothing is more irritating to musicians than carnivorous, self-styled critics - people who cannot or do not perform, but know exactly how things should be played. Frequently their pique stems from a sense of frustration over their own musical deficiencies. They read about music, attend concerts, listen to recordings, and proceed to tell everyone what Mr. Pianowski's shortcomings were. "Really, that coda to the first movement was much too fast. Did you hear that bass note he missed in the Rondo? Inexcusable. How could anyone play the theme so coldly? It should throb with emotion." Ah, yes, like the carnivore they can rend the artist apart and destroy beauty but never create it themselves.

The dedicated amateur who makes good use of the piano in the home sympathizes with the performer, appreciates his problems, understands more of the composer's intentions, and thrills to a fine performance.

The person who played Chopin's *A-flat Polonaise* appreciates the technical difficulties of the introduction, knows the problems of tone and pedal control, has struggled to play those octaves in the middle part without falling off the bench in sheer exhaustion, and has pondered over why Chopin put in that quite foreign section just before the first theme reappears near the end. When the amateur hears an artist surmount all these vexatious passages and thrill the listener with the nobility, strength, and excitement of the piece, here is reward indeed. The novice can hardly wait to get home to his piano to try some of those wonderful effects that cannot really be as hard as they appeared. It seemed so simple when the artist played it.

Some scoffers disapprove of performing great music unless one is on an artist's level. Why? Should an enthusiastic amateur painter turn all his pictures to the wall because they don't compare with Raphael's masterpieces?

I say let the amateur try it. True, his playing will not sound like that of the artist, but there is that great bond in music. He and Rubinstein have played the same piece. Paderewski thrilled his audiences with it years ago, Liszt played it with great success and helped launch Chopin's career as a composer, many fine artists have recorded it, and now he or she, the amateur, is playing it.

I realize that not everyone has a piano. If none is available, it is a good idea to seek out some instrument to conquer, or sing in a chorus or church choir. One should choose an instrument they like and get the advice of a good teacher as to their chances of playing it well enough to enjoy it. For example, it's not such a good idea to choose a harp because it looks so lovely to run fingers over the strings and produce those heavenly sounds, unless a person has a fine sense of pitch and is willing to have callouses on the fingers.

A cellist friend of ours was asked why she chose an instrument that is so awkward to transport. Sheepishly, she replied, "My music teacher in school thought I had some talent and asked if I could get a piccolo to play in the school orchestra. Mother went to the local music store to price instruments. To her dismay, a little tiny piccolo cost almost as much as a nice big student cello, and her practical nature won out. She bought the mellow-toned cello, and to this day I'm a cellist."

Children's Practice. If there is a piano in your house, a big question is how to interest your children in playing really well. To play well requires practice, and therein lies the difficulty. Children love to be active at an early age, and the time for practicing the piano seems to be one of comparative inactivity, though it really requires the greatest concentration and use of faculties. All the funny stories and cartoons about Junior's cries to escape practice have probably had their origin in some teacher's experience.

One of the best excuses given to me came from a little boy aged seven, whom we shall call Charley. He had very little interest in music, practiced the minimum amount of time, and only my regard for his mother's burning desire that he have some knowledge of music kept him on my list. One particular Saturday morning, he apologized for his lack of preparation and said, "I had a friend visiting me this week and he kept bothering me so I couldn't practice. He walked on the piano."

I looked properly horrified and said that never before had I heard of such a thing. With righteous indignation he continued, "Yes, and he walked on the piano with his shoes on. When I walk on the piano I always take my shoes off." I thought I'd heard all the alibis in the book, but that was a new one, and I'm sure I'll hear more.

Children are all different. There are some who love music and the piano enough to practice before school, gladly miss some playtime to practice after school, and just wait for the opportunity to play for family and friends. Their talent may range from a small spark to a great and consuming fire, but if the desire and joy in music is there, we are happy.

One of my most beloved young students started piano lessons at the age of five, which, in my opinion, is usually much too young for the average child. In this case, when the mother, a fine musician herself, pleaded with me at least to hear her, I succumbed to her charm, intelligence and talent. For one year my little student would come in with Mommy, one carrying a special box, the other a telephone book. The box was a rest for the little feet that couldn't reach the floor, and the telephone book was to sit on so she could reach the keys. What fun we had. Within the year little pieces of Mozart and Bach became her favorites. Her hands fit the keyboard as naturally as rivers flow to the ocean; every finger was right. Her melodies sang, her phrasing was a joy.

This child was ready for music. Her greatest punishment at home, rarely used, was to be told she couldn't practice for a certain period. Three years later her standard musical fare was Bach Inventions, Schubert Dances, Mozart Sonatas, and some contemporary music, as well as scales, arpeggios, and duets. Her mother helped tremendously. It was the type of situation teachers dream of. She was a joy, but definitely the exception rather than the rule.

Parents and teachers alike must learn to bear with certain imperfections in music study as in other phases of life. Many children like listening to music, learning about it, but they are really not ready to concentrate sufficiently to perfect their playing. Above all we must not kill that love of music. Charley's walking on the piano does not meet with my approval, but I do believe children should be allowed to play the piano keys from the time they can toddle. If you can't stand the scratches on the finish, get an old used upright, and put it someplace where it is accessible. Put it in the kitchen, the dining room, or anyplace so that the child can experiment with sound.

For her 7th grade home economics class, our daughter Becky was asked to draw a floor plan of her bedroom and determine how best to arrange the furniture. After working on it, she commented that it was difficult to find the best spot for the grand piano, but she didn't want it moved out - heaven forbid! (We figured no other students faced that problem.)

Between Charley and my gifted five-year-old student there are thousands of children who can be encouraged to play the piano well, and perhaps later study another instrument. Of course, if either or both parents play, that is the greatest help and inspiration, providing ambition doesn't become too dominating. Let the development come naturally. We cannot force any phase of physical, emotional or mental development without risking serious consequences, so let music develop at its natural rate and remember that it can be a lifetime pleasure if properly nurtured.

An adult student is not forced to study music and so manages to fit in the practice time whenever possible. However, the average child is easily distracted from practice. Just let a friend suggest playing ball or riding bicycles or any other thing that children love to do, and the piano becomes an enemy. If I knew a good formula for making practice more important I should deserve a niche in the Hall of Fame. I don't have a solution that fits every student, but I do know a few ways that have worked for some.

The system that worked for sister Sue may not do a thing for brother Carl. If you find a plan that works, stay with it. If interest lags, try a new system. It's as Edison said after another failure in one of his many inventions, "I now know of five thousand things that won't work."

At the top of the list of things that won't work for getting children to practice are the following rationales from well-meaning parents:

"But Alice, I never had the chance to study piano as a child. We've worked so hard and now can give you opportunities we didn't have. How can you be so indifferent?"

"Eddie, if I let you stop your lessons now you will regret it all your life. Some day you will reproach me for not making you go on."

"If Ella can find time to practice and play so well, why can't you?"

"When we bought the piano you were so thrilled and practiced so much. If you don't do better we'll just sell the piano."

Most children are not remotely interested in regrets that might assail them twenty years later. Though they love their parents, they are usually not interested in hardships their parents may have endured earlier. They are realistic. Today their parents have a nice home, good cars, and spend money for many things. It surely isn't breaking them up to pay for music lessons, so why worry? These aren't little monsters; they are children, and we shouldn't expect them to behave like adults.

If you want the piano in the house really used, here are a few strategies that have been successful in many cases:

1. Encourage your child to practice by listening to him. Sit in the room part of the time. If at all possible, comment on the good and bad features of the playing, particularly the good. If you are busy in another part of the house, comment from afar.

2. If possible, have a regular practice time set up. Sometimes this is difficult, but we are creatures of habit and the average child is happier having a regular time for practice.

3. Keep the piano in tune. It maybe old and battered, but if it is out of tune it is really harmful to a child's ear.

4. Choose the music teacher with care. A good teacher should love children, be able to interest them in music, be a good performer, have an attractive personality, and be devoted to music. I have known excellent teachers who have no music degree, some young, some old, some strict, and some gently persuasive.

There is no rule by which you find a good music teacher for your child. When you do, the teacher will have good suggestions for practice methods. It is important to work with the teacher.

If a child learns to love music, enjoys his lessons (though he may not enjoy practicing), has interest in listening to music and learning about musicians, and improves in his playing, he has a good teacher. Most good teachers are very busy, so start looking before your child is ready to start.

6. If your child wants to experiment at the piano, let him do it. Practice first, then "doodle."

7. All practicing need not be done at one time. Some students prefer to do each day's practice all at one time, while others prefer several short periods. When several children in the same family are studying, schedules need to be worked out.

8. Ask the teacher to write assignments in a notebook. Most teachers do as it saves confusion at home.

9. Occasionally, with the teacher's permission, sit in on a lesson. A parent can be more helpful if he knows what the teacher is trying to do.

10. Practice is work that can help develop a healthy attitude and satisfaction in overcoming difficulties.

Group Lessons. In recent years there has been a great advance in the number of teachers offering group lessons, or class piano, in the schools or private studios. I like group lessons, but, like all good ideas, it does not work for everyone, so I use both methods of teaching.

I like to start beginners in groups of three or four. They also have some individual lessons with a young assistant. Some children love it and the progress is excellent. Others don't like it at first but then begin to enjoy it. Some never adjust to it, and if they are talented, private lessons are a must.

It's normally impossible to find three or four students near the same age, with fairly equal ability and intelligence. However, we can usually find three or four who are near enough the same level, who like each other, and who enjoy working together.

The advantages of teaching in groups are many:

1. The financial outlay is not as great for the family.

2. For the teacher, missed lessons are not the usual bugbear. Rarely are three or four people ill or away at the same time, so time is well utilized.

3. Rhythmic playing is a must. Sometimes, after trying a new piece together with everyone counting - including the teacher - there are rhythmic errors, and sometimes everyone finishes at a different time. At that point some student usually says, "I can play it much better alone." That is the perfect opportunity for the teacher to ask, "Do you know why? Because when you play alone you take more time on difficult spots and hurry the easy ones." So the group tries again. If time permits, the students with problems may be heard individually.

4. With children and adults as well, it's fun to play together. Hilarity is usual when it's been so bad that it's ridiculous. That's better than having the tragic feeling of having failed in playing.

5. Students have to listen. Sometimes a student gets out of time, loses the place, listens, and then comes in several bars

later at the right time. That student has learned to follow the harmony, melody and rhythm. That is the most important skill.

6. The simplest piece must say something, so the mood is often discussed. One student may say, "This sounds like a storm, then it's quiet, and then it ends with more storm." Another may think it's a battle, with thoughts of home in the quiet part, before the battle resumes. The same piece of music can suggest many different pictures or stories to different students.

I remember asking one boy what the bombastic *Majesty of the Deep* meant to him. He replied, "fish." He must have meant a whale. The same boy, when asked if he knew what a "chorale" was promptly replied, "A place in the west where they keep horses." Teaching is never dull.

7. Usually when one student plays alone and the others listen, their criticism is constructive. Some are reluctant to criticize a friend, others are too eager to find faults, but generally there is a good attitude with youngsters and adults alike. For example, if a player has difficulty in playing a certain passage smoothly, the teacher may ask, "Annie, did you have a problem there too?" "I certainly did," replies Annie, "but I can play it better now because I went over it very slowly every day and now it's smoother."

Billy interrupts, "That wasn't the way I did it. I worked on it hands alone first, then put hands together." After each played the passage well, who's to say one was right and the other wrong? There are many ways to practice.

8. Sociability of the group is another big factor. If there are personality clashes, perhaps one student could be changed to another group. Occasionally good friends do not fit into a group well and sometimes strangers become good friends.

Generally the students enjoy each other and quickly recognize the musical good and bad traits of each player. They learn so much from each other.

9. Technic is so much more interesting in groups. We can compare the value of different touches, etc. In playing scales and arpeggios, one student usually excels and the others feel obliged to keep up.

Individual Lessons. We know that each pianist has different ideas and talents, and there are times when individual lessons provide the proper course to follow.

1. The student's individual talents should be developed so that after a certain length of time in group lessons there is a definite need for private lessons.

2. Shyness is a factor. Some students are hesitant to advance their ideas in a group but would talk freely to a teacher.

3. Most students have a certain competitive spirit, but not everyone. I've seen students wilt and do less and less if there is an overly aggressive person in the group. One or two teams of adults had to be dissolved because of the dominating personality of one member who played so loudly and drove the others to withdraw and play softer and softer. The balance became so bad that we had to find other players with which to team them.

4. Lesson time for a lesson shared among three or four persons instead of one cannot possibly allow as much individual attention.

5. There are physical differences. A partially deaf child or adult is lost in a group.

6. Psychologically there are certain factors that make private lessons a must. For example, someone recovering from a personal tragedy may take up music for its therapeutic value, and may need time to play and talk to the teacher alone.

I have had students come to a lesson pale with exhaustion, troubled over some personal difficulty or upset over making an important decision and tell me they haven't been able to practice. This is the time for me to let the student talk and then play something for me. At the end of the lesson, the student usually leaves relaxed and refreshed after this contact with music. This is not possible with groups.

7. As for the teacher, group lessons are much more demanding. In the allotted time, musical problems must be solved for several students, the attention of every student must be maintained, and in some cases there are discipline problems. There is the talker, the one who keeps drumming on his piano while another plays, the one who thinks he knows the answers to every question and is usually wrong, or the complainer, who doesn't like most of the music assigned, etc. Individually these problems can be solved more easily. In groups they are more wearing.

The best solution is a combination of group and private lessons. This cannot always be arranged, but it is ideal.

From Generation to Generation. When one starts to study piano as a child, he expects to progress through the years and become more proficient with practice and study. Most parents are pleased at any evidence of musical talent and make many sacrifices to encourage a child in his study of music. Many of them have no great aspirations other than giving a child a hobby that is enduring, helpful, fun, and a means of developing patience and coordination. There are a few exceptions. The most helpful parents are those with some musical education. Sometimes they reluctantly admit that they studied five years and can't play anything, or they really expected to concertize but got married instead, or a determined mother made her children practice and they hated it. Regardless of their background, they all wish to give their children this chance of learning to play music. It must have meant something to them, and they are always hopeful that their children will benefit from the experience more than they did.

Then there are those wonderful second-generation students. What a joy to music teachers to teach a child of a former student, to use the same music mother or father studied before, to correct a wrong note in the score and let the child in on a secret. "See that mark? Your mother missed that same note twenty years ago." Also, the second-generation musician can often see penciled in, "Practice more slowly," "Watch your fingering," "Check your notes," or "Less pedal." The advice is still good years later. I find children eager to learn about their parents' former life. Suddenly they are not just older people; they too were young, made mistakes, and practiced or didn't practice. Music used a second time is quite revealing. Toys and books can't tell quite the same story as marks on music.

What a thrill to play a recital piece that a parent had played - particularly if the performance comes off well. It is also a great joy to play duets with a parent. The wonderful common bond of music brings everyone together.

Occasionally our recitals have had family participation as a feature. Many teachers do this for obvious reasons. Children love the feeling of sharing some experiences with parents, and mothers are more tolerant of daughter's missed note if she has just missed one herself. A few experiences from these recitals stand out in my mind.

What a jolly time there was when we had a family trio of piano, cello, and violin. Junior was at the piano and finished several measures before his parents. I still laugh over Mary's attempt to accompany her mother who was singing the Bach-Gounod *Ave Maria*. The tempo became so slow that mother ended up gasping for breath. Nor shall I ever forget a son accompanying his father's flute solo. After half a page Junior stopped, glared at his father, a distinguished professor, and said, "We aren't together. You made a mistake. We might as well start over." They did, and the second time was successful.

Disasters do not occur in all performances. Some are exceptionally fine. As one father said after a strenuous duet that came off well, "I practiced more in the last month than I have in 25 years, but it was worth it."

Professional musicians are not always the most helpful. Their ideals may be so high that unless they are also teachers they become impatient with children's mistakes. Furthermore, the life of a professional performer or conductor is strenuous and demanding; he must always produce and is not so sympathetic to mistakes as a friend might be.

A symphony player of our acquaintance came home after five hours of strenuous rehearsing followed by four hours of teaching. His talented daughter was practicing at the piano, and upstairs his son was playing the trumpet quite well. He listened a few moments, then said to his wife, "Tell Sally she can keep on playing the piano - just for fun - but tell Johnny to put the trumpet away. I don't want to hear it again. He's too good, and he might want to become a musician, heaven help him!" Both daughter and son became fine professional musicians.

That was a temporary mood, for most musicians would not exchange their lives for any other. They may envy the money an executive earns, or wish for a new car like the doctor has, but that is only human nature. Once music has hold of a person it is hard to break the spell.

Every Pianist a Good Sight Reader. Anyone who really wants to enjoy making music must learn to sight read well. Just as one reads books of travel, biography, or fiction, and explores new territory wondering what is over the next mountain, one can approach music in that same frame of mind. It involves training, muscular skill, intellectual skill, and willingness to forge ahead regardless of the sound.

If a pianist has laboriously sight read Bach chorales in duet form, easy four-hand arrangements of little dances, two-part inventions, or the two-piano eight-hand version of the Bach *Suite in D Major*, no matter how badly he has performed, he is better equipped to study the *Little Preludes and Fugues*, or to listen to the *B minor Mass*.

The best possible way to improve one's reading is by playing in groups. For pianists, playing duets on one piano is very helpful, but even better is four players on two pianos with a fifth acting as a guide or referee, whichever term seems fitting. Start with fairly easy music, set a comfortable tempo and stay with it. It is quite helpful to spend a few minutes studying the part to be played. Check the key, rhythm, tempo, pattern, and places where suddenly something changes melodically or rhythmically.

The most important rule is to keep moving. Whether there are two six-year-olds or four pianists of assorted ages from thirty to seventy, once you start, proceed. In the first session of this kind, a novice sight reader frequently makes a mistake, stops and says, "I played something wrong. I'm lost." The guide or referee points to the place where the player should be and whispers fiercely, "Go on - one - two - three - catch it on one of the next measures." "The others proceed just as though no one had gone overboard and with good luck two pages get finished. After several experiences of this kind, the novice soon learns to hang on at all costs, and the group doesn't stop again unless three out of the four are in different places and Haydn begins to sound like Schoenberg.

There is nothing more exhilarating than to forge ahead through a movement of a symphony, working hard, perspiring, listening, counting, and finally ending a section together. A number of adult students count these hours as purest gold. Sometimes there is no other time for practice in a busy life than sight reading. This is real music making.

Practicing and working out details as I have outlined above is comparable to studying a language or history. One can memorize French grammar and vocabulary by dint of hard mental effort and drill, but one learns to speak French fluently only by listening to the language and speaking it in regular conversations with others who speak it.

With perseverance anyone can improve reading skills. How does it sound? Usually pretty terrible at times, particularly in the early stages. Just don't expect musical miracles. But once basic sight reading skills are achieved, one can begin to produce pleasing music. The eye can now take in dynamics, the ear listens for a melody, and the player gradually becomes adept at getting back in after falling out.

Even in solo playing there are no miracles. Professional and amateur musicians alike recognize that fact. A person might start studying Mozart's *Sonata in C Major*. At first it does not sound very good, but it can be put aside for quite a while, even a year or more, while the student reads other Mozart compositions, gains technical proficiency, listens to recordings, learns about Mozart's life, and then gets back to the *C Major Sonata*. This procedure can be done over and over. There is no end to perfecting a great piece. It can always be played better.

In one master class, Victor Babin said solemnly to a graduate student who had just performed a Beethoven sonata, "If you live to be a hundred you could never play that as beautifully as it should be played. No performer is as great as the music."

I remember some years ago a group of four earnest ladies had slowly plowed their way through Mendelssohn's *Italian Symphony*. Two weeks later two of these women were at a symphony concert. As the orchestra went into the third movement, one lady said in an awed whisper, "Isn't that the piece we played last time in quartet?" Her friend replied, "I believe it is," and they beamed proudly. It sounded somewhat different, but it was their piece.

The Adult Beginner. Too many adults who start music study become discouraged at their slow progress. There are many people who are successful in their chosen fields, and accustomed to success. They love music, go to concerts, listen to fine recordings and want to play the piano. They hunt up a good teacher who explains the keyboard and notation. With complete confidence in their ability to comprehend their instructions, they go home to practice enthusiastically.

Then it starts. They mean to play a C and then E, but the nasty finger plays D. They go over this a number of times till finally it is right. They go on, come back, and instead of D they hit E. For intelligent people, this is maddening. If one knows something, why does one do the wrong thing? Be patient. Sooner or later the student will play E where it is meant to be, but perfection will take time. Anyone who says playing the piano is easy is misguided. It is easier for some than others, but easy? No! It is a constant challenge.

Which is your weakest finger? The fourth, of course. That is why your fourth and fifth fingers take so much extra practice before they even begin to react properly. No one even notices this weakness until he starts to play and then begins to see why Schuman invented the pulley to pull the fourth finger higher and thus give it strength. Unfortunately Schuman ruined his finger, but one can sympathize with his efforts.

There is also the adult who is accustomed to speaking before groups with the greatest of ease. After months of laboring at the piano, he is ready to perform a one-page piece, Schumann's *Wild Horseman*, for a group of 15 fellow students. He goes to the piano, sits down, and looks at the keyboard, which suddenly seems to swallow him up. His legs shake, his fingers can't locate the right notes, he perspires and thinks, "Why did I ever get into this?" With head swimming, he somehow locates the first notes and away he goes, usually gaining confidence as he proceeds. It's over. His friends are astonished and pleased at his accomplishments, and suddenly, he knows how it felt to climb Mt. Everest. This is really living, this is a true challenge in our so-called "soft' modern living.

Strangely enough, after a student has lived through the first performance, he is willing to try again. Sometimes with a fellow student or students he finds it a bit less wearing on his nerves, and practicing with someone else is fun. If someone else in the family plays another instrument or sings, accompanying is another new experience. An accompanist must be flexible and follow the soloist, no matter how crooked the way. It's a good idea to try to get some experience in accompanying because one never knows when he might unexpectedly be called on to accompany.

It isn't only the beginner who has unexpected or unusual experiences. In our family we try to refer to them as "good experiences." In fact, the term "good experience" has become a byword.

When our daughter Dorothy Katherine was studying at Eastman, she wrote an account of being drafted to play for her first Jewish service on 15 minutes' notice. The organist couldn't see the choir, the music was complex, and someone poked her when it was time to play and give the pitch to the choir. Unfortunately, in the first response, that note on the organ wouldn't sound, so she sang it. I reminded her that it was "good experience."

Years ago, one of my talented students was asked to play at a church gathering. As he sat down at the battered upright, he wondered why an elderly lady was sitting right next to him. He soon found out as he played. About twelve different keys stuck. The lady's function was to reach under his hands and push them up again. Perhaps this "good experience" helped to give him poise when he later played with the Cincinnati and Chicago Symphony Orchestras.

My second appearance with our College Symphony was marked by a weird experience. As we neared the end of the second movement of the concerto, I heard a loud noise. The conductor kept beating as he peered out into the audience. The players stole glances over their music and I played on until I had a long enough rest to look out. Imagine seeing a woman's feet as she was being carried out after fainting. I almost fainted myself. But my motto of "good experience" kept my seat firmly glued to the piano bench and my eyes to the director's baton.

Art is Long - and Difficult. Every student has a burning desire to master some great piece that he loves. What if it takes a year, or even two years? Whenever he can really play that piece with some assurance, precision and taste, life will be more worthwhile. He too will discover that there is always another mountain to go over. What satisfied him ten years ago isn't good enough today. He has learned more and is now more critical of his playing than he used to be. Frustrating? A little, but this is another challenge. Relearn it, improve it, and now there comes that yearning to at least try the Schumann *Concerto* or some other favorite. So the process starts again, ever new and interesting to both student and teacher.

From childhood on it's the same. The six-year-old, with missing front teeth, hears a nine-year-old play Beethoven's *Für Elise* at a recital. He loves it and several years later he is ready to try it.

Some pieces are too difficult at certain stages of development, and teachers must exercise restraint. Within reason it is good to try a difficult piece that one aches to play. No one grows unless he has fresh incentive, greater difficulties, and new ideas to absorb.

I remember one high school student who wished to play the *"Pathétique" Sonata* of Beethoven. He liked the first movement especially, and since he was bright and talented (although lazy) we started the piece with fear and trembling. He persevered for a year, determined to conquer it. Never before had he shown such desire to see it through.

When Percy Grainger paid one of his occasional visits to Cincinnati for a concert, he held master classes for adults and teenagers. My student was willing to be led to the slaughter, and slaughter it was. Before an artist, as well as a group of fellow students all mistakes seem magnified. Some things about his playing were good, but too many were not. As I expected, his performance was justly criticized on all counts.

After the class, I looked in his direction and saw disappointment written on his face. He loved that piece, he had tried hard, he did feel it, and he had worked more than ever before, but not enough. We talked it over, and to the relief of a devoted mother, we shelved Mr. Beethoven and all his "pathetic" ideas for an indefinite period.

Two years later Mr. Grainger was again scheduled to come for a concert and lessons. As I lined up various performers I asked this boy, hesitantly, "Would you like to play again in Mr. Grainger's class?" His eyes lit up with the fire of battle as he said quickly, "Yes, I certainly do, and I want to play the *'Pathétique'* again. I know I can do better." So again we started, but now it was different. He was determined to prove something to himself, his family, me, and especially Percy Grainger. This time he worked with greater understanding, alert to observe every mark, and listening to his dynamics, melody, and clarity.

Came the cold winter day of the class. Teenagers arrived early at the lovely home of one of my students, where a cheery fire in the fireplaces generated warmth and even encouragement. They talked in rather hushed tones until Mr. Grainger arrived. He greeted them warmly and the class began. Most of these teenagers had never played in such a class before. Those from last year were better equipped to stand the strain of playing before an artist, and having all their faults pointed out before a group of fellow students. I admired their courage.

The morning flew by, and soon this boy was asked to play. As he played, I became aware that his playing was much better than before. It was steadier, cleaner, more melodic, and controlled yet inspired. I whispered a little prayer on his behalf because it was so important to him.

After he finished, Mr. Grainger said in a rather surprised and pleased way, "Didn't you play this for me before?" "Yes, sir," he replied tensely. "How much you have improved," said Mr. Grainger. "This is quite miraculous. It sounds so much better in every way."

The smile that spread over that boy's face was beautiful to behold, and I caught myself grinning like Alice's Cheshire Cat. This was reward indeed, and everyone who had been present before felt a sense of gratification, too. What an important lesson in life - as well as music: Don't be discouraged by one failure, or even more. Pick yourself up, determine to prove your worth, work harder than ever before, and you can do it. Music has a way of building character as well as technique, and I firmly believe that people who love music tend to be interesting, kind people.

I often hear a dissenting voice saying, "Musicians are nuts. They aren't like normal people. They do the craziest things." Maybe, but if so, I'm glad I'm one of the nuts!

The Many Moods of Music. We hear much about music therapy in mental hospitals, how it is used to speed up production in factories and even to accelerate the growth of plants. That is all fine indeed, and that piano in your house can help you and your family to a better life.

One mother whose husband was being transferred to South America said, "Don't worry about Gail's music. She will study wherever we are. We are allowed to take a certain weight of household goods, and believe me our piano and books go first.

We can sit or sleep on the floor, but books and a piano are a must."

Loss of a loved one makes music alien for some. It's so very close to a person's emotions and associations to be much help for some time, but there it is waiting to help. I've seen people come back to it gradually. A mother whose only son had died, the young wife whose husband was killed in an auto accident, the daughter whose father had deserted the family - I could go on and on. But sooner or later, one becomes able to go back to music, listen to it, work with it and be comforted by it. This is not an idle pedantic theory held by a teacher. I've seen the therapeutic value of music again and again.

Some people have moods which they like to match at the piano. As one lady put it, "When I'm mad at the children, the washer breaks down, and the rabbits have dug up my tulip bulbs, I don't blow my top. I go to the piano and really bang out Chopin's *'g minor Prelude'*. It may not sound great, but boy, it's good for my nerves."

I defy anyone to spend an hour on the Clementi *Sonatina No. 1 in C* or Haydn's *D Major Sonata*, or Bach's *Gigue* and *Allemande* from the *B-flat Partita* and remain troubled or sad. The music is cheerful and alive, and seems to say that even though life one or two hundred years ago was also confused and full of wars and greed, one can still think about the good things. One is alive. That's something! The sun rises and sets in all its beauty, the majestic mountains still reach for the sky, the mighty oceans are filled with tremendous waves, people still dance and sing, they paint, they write, they love, they produce children, so focus on music that brings you joy and you'll feel better.

All this does not come to a student immediately. As he works with the notes, rhythm, dynamics, phrasing and touches, little by little the mood reaches out and engulfs him. Working with any true art or expression of beauty is good. Just as the composer worked lovingly over every note, so should the student. Easy? No! Rewarding? Yes!

As well as joy, there is humor in music. Haven't you heard a ripple of laughter from an audience that has just heard Debussy's *Golliwog's Cake Walk* or Dukas' *Sorcerer's Apprentice* or Prokofiev's *Peter and the Wolf*?

In the realm of folk music, Percy Grainger's delightful *Country Gardens* and *Shepherd's Hey* are filled with lusty good humor of country people enjoying dancing in the open air. Even Schubert's lovely Viennese waltzes retain elements of the ländler, or country dances, from which they originated.

All of this music can be played on the piano, either in solo or duet versions, and they remind a person again of the stream of music flowing through the years from good old Bach through the nineteenth century into our day when jazz and rock provide most of the dance music. All types of music are interesting. A student should not be limited to just the romantic or contemporary schools.

Try everything. Art and literature have vastly different styles in each century, but the basic principles are the same. Talented people have expressed ideas and feelings in various forms, and if they are good, basic, and universal, they have survived.

Too much of our life is spent acquiring things and taking care of them. To be sure, things are necessary and a piano is really a thing. But just as a person is more than body, a piano is more than wood and metal. The spirit of music comes through the instrument and has the power to match one's mood or change it whenever it is played.

Whether one starts the study of music as a child or an adult, performs for a club, such as the Keyboard Club, or in Carnegie Hall, the study of music is ever opening up new vistas. With the study of music comes a sense of joy and that wonderful feeling of being linked with the great music and musicians of the past. Great music, like religion, gives one a feeling of permanence so vital in this ever-changing world. I know that music has enriched my life beyond measure, and the opportunity to share it with so many through performing and teaching is the greatest gift I could ever have hoped for.

Postlude: Reflections by Rebecca Shockley

Much has happened since this book was first published. I have updated what my mother wrote about my siblings and myself, and have added information about some significant events that were not included in the original version. But much more can be said about her extraordinary and productive life and career. Despite her busy schedule, she managed to continue performing at a high level for most of her life, even though there were many days when she could only squeeze in 30 minutes of practice at 7:30 a.m. before beginning a long day of teaching. She also continued to learn new music, study under great artists in master classes, and keep abreast of developments in pedagogy, attending workshops by well-known pedagogues such as Frances Clark, David Carr Glover, Guy Maier, and others. She also met with Raymond Burrows at Columbia University, and was impressed by his innovative and dynamic approach to class piano instruction. But in her early 80s she began to slow down.

After moving to a smaller house on Howell Ave. in 1980, she continued teaching a few students in her home. Fortunately, Karl was also living in Cincinnati at the time, and was able to help her a great deal. Along with Keyboard Club meetings, they occasionally performed together at his Unity Church. When she reached the point where he felt she was no longer safe living alone at home, he and Dorothy helped her relocate to Brookwood, a comfortable retirement home, for her final years.

In the year following her death in 1992, Dorothy, Karl and I decided to perform a "Payne Family Recital" in Cincinnati in her memory. The program consisted of works for two pianos, one piano-six hands, and solos, including a piece by Percy Grainger. This was so much fun that we decided to do it regularly and "take it on the road," giving recitals every other year after that until 2008. There were three performances of each recital – one in Cincinnati sponsored by the Keyboard Club, one at the University of South Carolina, where Dorothy served as Dean of the College of Music and Professor of Music Theory, and one at the University of Minnesota, where I was teaching. After Dorothy's death in 2010, Karl and I continued to perform together periodically on the Keyboard Club's annual fall recital by members.

In 2010, The Keyboard Club celebrated its 75th Anniversary with a Gala Concert. For this occasion, *Is There a Piano in the House?* was reprinted, and recordings of past Payne Family Recitals (and Mother's 1971 London Recital) were made available on CDs.

In 2013, I was invited to write an article about my mother for the Jan-Feb 2015 issue of *Clavier Companion*. I went through many boxes of clippings, photographs, programs, diplomas, letters (including ones from Percy and Ella Grainger, Vronsky and Babin, Tcherepnin, Goossens, and others), albums, and collections of tributes from Keyboard Club members gathered for the 25th, 40th, and 50th anniversaries of the club. From these I learned a lot about her beyond what was recorded in her memoirs, so I created a PowerPoint about her life and career to present at the start of the Keyboard Club fall recital in 2014. Afterward, Karl and I delivered several boxes of documents to the University of Cincinnati Library, which now houses the Dorothy S. Payne Archives. There are also archives of the Keyboard Club housed in the Cincinnati Historical Society collection at the Museum Center in Union Terminal.

Music Scholarships have long been an important part of the Keyboard Club's mission. Over the years, the Keyboard Club Scholarship Fund established in Mother's memory has grown substantially, and Karl began thinking about what more might be done with the funds. Working with the Greater Cincinnati Foundation, the Keyboard Club officers, and the development office of the University of Cincinnati, we have succeeded in establishing the Dorothy S. Payne Scholarship in Piano at the College-Conservatory of Music. The money will support an outstanding performer who demonstrates the passion for teaching and the ability to collaborate with others that were hallmarks of my mother's career. We expect the first such scholarship to be awarded in the Fall of 2018, and I feel certain that Mother would be pleased to know that these funds will help to support excellent piano teaching in the future.

APPENDIX I – DOROTHY PAYNE AS TEACHER
by Rebecca Shockley

Teaching Style and Philosophy. As a teacher, Mother was patient, kind and encouraging, and she never turned down a student who really wanted to learn, regardless of their ability level. She had a knack for finding the right piece for each student, and she could demonstrate any piece beautifully – or accompany a concerto at a moment's notice. When a student really needed to talk, she was a sympathetic listener. She encouraged ensemble playing – duets, duo-piano, and piano quartets - and felt that all her students should have regular opportunities to perform for their peers. She also used classes and group instruction.

Group Classes for Musicianship. Although Mother taught most of her students individually, she started some of her beginning students in small groups (with two grand pianos and an upright in her living room studio). She also offered regular classes to her students to enrich their curriculum. In a 1947 article for *Etude Magazine* entitled "Bringing Delight to Music Study," she described three different plans for her classes.

Musicianship Class, 1947

In the first plan, each student performed a solo, followed by peer critique and some ear training and/or performances by the teacher of pieces the students might like to learn. She then divided the class into two groups, with one group studying the score of a simple piece, and the other studying a set of musical questions and answers. After the two groups switched, students took turns sight reading the new piece, and everyone tried to answer the questions studied.

For the second plan, each child was given a new piece two weeks before the class to learn independently and perform for the class, either with or without the score. These classes also included ensemble sight reading at one or two pianos, experimenting with playing and hearing different dynamic levels, and a brief discussion of current musical events, radio programs, etc.

The third plan included a scale contest. Students were graded on fingering, smoothness, and accuracy, and prizes were awarded. She would then tell a musical story and ask students questions about the story. Then each student was given a simple solo to sight read, while the others gathered around and watched for errors. If someone noticed a mistake, the student had to stop playing and another went to the piano. The student who played the most measures without a mistake won a prize. At the end of the class, she would demonstrate a well known piece, first playing it poorly – missed notes, rhythms, balance, etc. – and asking the students to critique the performance. She would then play it again as beautifully as possible.

Refreshments were served after every gathering so that students and parents could relax and get to know each other.

Posters of Musical Terms. In 1954, Mother commissioned Paula Siehl, a student at Earlham College and a talented artist, to design some posters with appealing illustrations of musical terms. She used these in her musicianship classes to help students remember the terms, and students really enjoyed them. The posters were later adopted by the Cincinnati School Board for use in public school music classes. Below are some examples:

The Key Signature Carousel. Mother had a small carousel in her studio, with a horse on a pole for each major and minor key, going through the circle of fifths. Each time the student mastered a new scale, they were allowed to hang their name on the corresponding pole. She also had a set of small xylophones, which were used for ensemble playing in her group classes.

The Carousel with 24 keys, 1950

APPENDIX II – SELECTED PROGRAMS AND LETTERS

1918 recital by Dorothy Stolzenbach (age 13) and Elizabeth Henderson

Piano Recital

Dorothy Stolzenbach
Elizabeth Henderson

Pupils of Mrs. A. A. Henderson

Friday Evening, June 28th, 1918

at 8:30 o'clock

520 Wallace Avenue, Wilkinsburg, Pennsylvania

Sonata Pathetique, Op. 13 .... Beethoven
                  Dorothy Stolzenbach

Solfeggietto .... C. P. E. Bach
Invention in F .... J. S. Bach
Fantasia—D-Minor .... Mozart
                  Elizabeth Henderson

Pastoral with Variations .... Mozart
Kamennoi—Ostrow .... Rubinstein
                  Dorothy Stolzenbach

Barchetta .... Nevin
Shepherds and Shepherdesses .... Godard
Arabesque .... Schumann
                  Elizabeth Henderson

Loerley .... Seeling
Prelude, Op. 28, No. 17 .... Chopin
Novelette in F .... Schumann
                  Dorothy Stolzenbach

Butterfly .... Grieg
Birdling .... Grieg
Nocturne, Op. 32, No. 1 .... Chopin
                  Elizabeth Henderson

Duet—Andante from Fifth Symphony .... Beethoven
                  Dorothy Stolzenbach
                  Elizabeth Henderson

Recital by Dorothy Stolzenbach and Karl Payne, College of Music, 1926 (front)

Cincinnati College of Music
PRESENTS
DOROTHY STOLZENBACH, Pianist
FROM THE CLASS OF
ALBINO GORNO
ASSISTED BY
KARL A. PAYNE, Violinist
FROM THE CLASS OF
ADOLF HAHN
IN A
RECITAL
COLLEGE OF MUSIC AUDITORIUM
THURSDAY EVENING, MARCH 11, 1926
AT 8:15 O'CLOCK

YOU AND YOUR FRIENDS ARE CORDIALLY INVITED   (OVER)

Recital by Dorothy Stolzenbach and Karl Payne, College of Music, 1926 (back)

Program

Melody from "Orfeus" .... Gluck
1744-1787
  (Concert arrangement by Sgambati)

Prelude, Sarabande, Courante .... Bach
  (From Partita in G major)

Sarabande in A major .... Rameau
1683-1764
  (Concert transcription by MacDowell)

Andante Favorito in F major .... Beethoven

Preludes, Opus 28, Nos. 22, 21, 23
.... Chopin

Etude in E major, Opus 10, No. 3 .. Chopin

Etude in C sharp minor, Opus 10,
  No. 4 .... Chopin

Sonata for Violin and Piano .. César Franck
  Allegretto ben moderato
  Allegro
  Recitativo Fantasia
  Allegretto poco mosso

MISS STOLZENBACH—MR. PAYNE

The Dance of Puck .... Debussy
Footprints in the Snow .... Debussy
The Brooklet ...... Schubert-Rachmaninoff
Rhapsodie Hongroise No. 4 .... Liszt

Baldwin Piano Used.

College of Music Graduating Class, 1926

Dorothy Payne's Master's Degree, Cincinnati Conservatory, 1934

1948 Recital by Percy Grainger

1948 Recital by Percy Grainger, cont.

PART I

Two Pianos
ITALIAN CONCERTO . . . . Bach-Bauer
Mrs. Robert Pugh - Mrs. Edward Hodgetts

Voices, Strings and Piano
COLONIAL SONG . . . . . . Grainger
Jane Malaer-SOPRANO   John Alexander-TENOR
Mrs. Ralph Patton-PIANIST

Two Pianos
SPOON RIVER . . . . . . Grainger
Virginia Garrett Kelly   Jane Malaer

Women's Chorus
THE HUNTER IN HIS CAREER . . Grainger
Women's Chorus directed by Mildred Marsh Conner
Mary Giaccio-ACCOMPANIST

Two Pianos
GREEN BUSHES (Passacaglia) . . Grainger
Ann Marilyn Hess   Lucinda Robb Hess
Melva Thomas

INTERMISSION

PART II

Two Pianos
FUGUE in A Minor . . . . Bach-Grainger
Mrs. Matt Schaefer   Mrs. Frank Cappel
Lillian McKeever   Mrs. Ford Larrabee

Two Pianos and Harmonium
JUTISH MEDLEY . . . . . Grainger
Percy Grainger, Dorothy Stolzenbach Payne,
Mrs. Milton Tobin - PIANISTS
Linda Iacobucci Wellbaum-ORGANIST

1948 Recital by Percy Grainger, cont.

Two Pianos
    GROSSE FUGUE . . . . Beethoven-Bauer
        Percy Grainger-Dorothy Stolzenbach Payne

Voice
    TO ECHO. . . . . . Ella Grainger
        Jane Malaer-SOPRANO

    LOVE AT FIRST SIGHT. . . . Ella Grainger
        Jane Malaer and Women's Chorus

    CRYING FOR THE MOON. . . . Ella Grainger
        Mrs. Hugh Gregg
        Percy Grainger   Mrs. Ford Larrabee
                PIANISTS
        Mary Ann Roettle - Lucinda Robb Hess
            Catherine Fisher - MARIMBAS

    THE ONLY SON (Kipling) . . Percy Grainger
        John Alexander-TENOR
    (WITH PIANO, REED ORGAN, HARP AND STRINGS)

Piano and Strings
    HANDEL IN THE STRAND (Clog Dance)   Grainger
        Percy Grainger - PIANO

ASSISTING ARTISTS

Mrs. Oliver Perin   Mr. Karl Payne
        VIOLINISTS
Mr. Herman Wasserman
        VIOLIST
Mrs. R. D. Wilbur   Miss Myrtle Whitehead
        CELLISTS
Mr. John Alexander
        TENOR
Linda Iacobucci Wellbaum
        ORGANIST and HARPIST

1950 Recital by Percy Grainger

THE KEYBOARD CLUB

Presents

An Evening of Chamber Music

with

PERCY GRAINGER — Pianist-Composer
As Guest Artist and Director

Wednesday, April 26, 1950

8:15 P.M.

ART MUSEUM—EDEN PARK

1950 Recital by Percy Grainger, cont.

... PROGRAM ...

Two Pianos
    Fugue in A Minor..*Bach-Grainger*
        Mrs. Eric Stockton   Percy Grainger
        Mrs. Raymond Myer   Marjorie Simpson

Voices
    Playing on Heart Strings...*Ella Grainger*
        Mrs. Hugh Gregg, Contralto   Mr. Myron Hurney, Tenor
        and mixed chorus directed by Mildred Marsh Conner

Two Pianos
    Prelude in C Major...*Bach-Grainger*
        Mildred Miller   Virginia Gulino

Four Solovoxes
    Fugue in C Major..*Bach-Grainger*
        Nancy Fuldner   Percy Grainger
        Mrs. Adrian Lammers   Mrs. Reul Smith

Four Solovoxes
    Prelude in E Major...*Bach-Grainger*
        Mrs. Edward Kieffer   Mrs. H. C. Beekley
        Mrs. Thomas Ryan   Percy Grainger

Two Pianos
    Fugue in E Major...*Bach-Grainger*
        Percy Grainger   Mrs. Frank Pfefferle
        Mrs. Frank Cappel   Mrs. Peter Wilshire

Voice
    Sprig of Thyme...*Grainger*
    Willow Willow...*Grainger*
        Miss Jane Malaer, Soprano
        (with string accompaniment)

Two Pianos
    Thamar ....*Balikireff*
        Anne Marilyn Hess   Ann Gatch
        Melva Thomas   Mrs. Milton Tobin

        — INTERMISSION —

1950 Recital by Percy Grainger, cont.

String Quintette   (World Premier)
  Movement for Strings..................................*Balfour Gardiner-Grainger*
    Mr. Karl Payne, Violin   Mrs. Edward Sieber, Viola
    Mrs. Oliver Perin, Violin   Patricia Ann Hunt, Cello
         Mrs. Thomas E. Hall, Cello

Voices, Strings, Marimbas and Piano   (World Premier)
  The Lonely Desert Man Sees the Happy Tribes........................*Grainger*
         Ella Grainger, Mezzo Soprano
         John Alexander, Tenor
         Dewey Owens, Baritone

Four Solovoxes
  Fugue in D Sharp Major..*Bach-Grainger*
    Mrs. Archibald Allen   Mrs. Ford Larrabee
    Percy Grainger   Lucinda Robb Hess

Voice
  Barbry Allen..*Grainger*
         Dewey Owens, Baritone

Two Pianos
  Blithe Bells...*Bach-Grainger*
  Molly on the Shore..*Grainger*
    Percy Grainger   Dorothy Stolzenbach Payne

Voices, Strings, Marimbas, Oboe
  Random Round..*Grainger*
         Petronella Trimbur Kiely, Soprano
         Mrs. Hugh Gregg, Contralto
         Mr. Myron Hurney, Tenor

Voice
  Pretty Maid Milkng A Cow...*Grainger*
  Reiver's Neck Verse...*Grainger*
         John Alexander, Tenor

Two Pianos
  Brisk Young Sailor } from Lincolnshire Posy..........................*Grainger*
  Harkstow Grange   }
    Mrs. Robert Pugh   Lucinda Robb Hess

Two Pianos and Chorus
  The Lost Lady Found—from Lincolnshire Posy.....................*Grainger*
    Mrs. Robert Pugh   Lucinda Robb Hess

         Mary Ann Roettle—Guest Marimba Player

               Baldwin Pianos

1958 Recital by Percy Grainger

THE KEYBOARD CLUB
AND
GERMAN DEPARTMENT
OF THE UNIVERSITY OF CINCINNATI

PRESENT

PERCY GRAINGER
COMPOSER - PIANIST

IN

A PROGRAM OF TWO PIANO MUSIC

WITH

DOROTHY STOLZENBACH PAYNE

ASSISTED BY

MEMBERS OF THE KEYBOARD CLUB

AT

WILSON AUDITORIUM

TUESDAY, MARCH 11TH, 1958 AT 8:15 P.M.

1958 Recital by Percy Grainger, cont.

TWO PIANOS - EIGHT HANDS

Fugue in A Minor from
"The Well Tempered Clavichord" .... Bach-Grainger

    Mrs Robert Hopkins .... Mrs. Robert Siegfried
    Mrs. Reuel Smith .... Mrs. Ray Shilling

Concerto for Piano .... Delius

PERCY GRAINGER

(Orchestral part on second piano played by ..... Dorothy Stolzenbach Payne
                                                                Sylvia Kleve Sheblessy

Two Symphonic Dances .... Cyril Scott
    Allegro con brio
        Andante Sostenuto e sempre molto cantabile

Scherzo .... Daniel Gregory Mason
    Percy Grainger .... Dorothy Stolzenbach Payne

INTERMISSION

1958 Recital by Percy Grainger, cont.

Fantasy on "Porgy and Bess" .... Gershwin - Grainger

Percy Grainger .... Dorothy Stolzenbach Payne

TWO PIANOS - SIX HANDS

Random Round .... Grainger

    Mrs. Robert Pugh .... Mrs. Elmer Hess

    Mrs. Ranald West .... Mrs. Ford Larrabee

    Mrs. Luke Jacobs .... Mrs. Raymond P. Myers

Spinning Song from "Pelleas and Mélissande" .... Fauré

Lincolnshire Posy .... arranged by Percy Grainger

    Dublin Bay

    Harkstow Grange

    The Lost Lady Found

Percy Grainger .... Dorothy Stolzenbach Payne

London Recital by Dorothy Payne, 1971

Greater London Council
PURCELL ROOM
Director: John Denison CBE

Tuesday
23 November 1971
at 7.30 p.m.

The Percy Grainger Library Society
presents

DOROTHY STOLZENBACH PAYNE piano

Management: BASIL DOUGLAS LTD.
8 St. George's Terrace, London NW1 8XJ (01-722 7142)

TICKETS: All at 50p.
available 23 October from Box Office, Royal Festival Hall, London SE1 8XX
(01-928 3191)

London Recital by Dorothy Payne, 1971, cont.

PROGRAMME

The Carman's Whistle	BYRD/GRAINGER
Now, O now, we needs must part	DOWLAND/GRAINGER
Prelude and Fugue in B flat major *(Well Tempered Klavier, Book I)*	BACH (1685-1750)
Spoon River *(American folk tune)* One more day, my John *(English sea chanty)* Shepherd's Hey *(Morris dance tune)*	PERCY GRAINGER 1882-1961
Nocturne, Opus 15 No. 2 Fantasy, Opus 49	CHOPIN (1810-1849

INTERVAL

Poissons d'or	DEBUSSY (1862-1918)
Des pas sur la neige Jeux d'eau	RAVEL (1875-1937)
Ballade, Opus 24	GRIEG (1843-1907)
Colonial Song The Hunter in his Career *(Old English popular song)*	GRAINGER

Although PERCY GRAINGER was not a teacher of piano in the ordinary sense, he sometimes gave 'master' instruction to young artists of promise. One such artist was DOROTHY STOLZENBACH PAYNE, and therefore, to commemorate the tenth anniversary of Grainger's death, the Percy Grainger Library Society of New York have arranged for her to give this recital, in which she will play music by Grainger and by other composers which she studied with him. The Library Society say: "We find her playing 'documentary', in the sense that she sounds almost as if he himself were playing."

Her programme will interest pianists, piano teachers, and all those who interest themselves in the art of piano playing.

Miss Payne lives and teaches in Cincinnati, where she has been a member of the Conservatory Faculty and staff pianist with the Symphony Orchestra.

Recital by Dorothy Payne, Canton, OH, ca. 1930

Recital by Louis Kohnop, age 12, 1932

Programs from her College Scrapbook (1923-1927)

Mother saved programs from the concerts and recitals she heard at the College:

1923: Anna Pavlova, Guy Maier (2-piano), Mary Garden.

1924: Marcel Dupré, Ignaz Friedman, Vladimir de Pachmann, Sergei Rachmaninoff, Jascha Heifitz, Carl Flesch, Harold Bauer, Ignaz Paderewski, Nicolai Medtner, Max Rosen (violin). Also operas: Tannhaüser, Mme Butterfly, Boris Goudunov.

1925: Gitta Gradova, Myra Hess, Sergei Rachmaninoff, Alfredo Casella (conductor and pianist on all Casella program), John Phillip Sousa, Percy Grainger, Igor Stravinsky (conducting all-Stravinsky concert).

1926: CSO season: Walter Gieseking, Josef Szigeti, Alfred Cortot, Lauritz Melchior, Efrem Zimbalist, Hans Kindler (cello). [She was also hired by the NY manager of John Corigliano, Sr., Concertmaster, NY Philharmonic, to accompany him in a program at Eastern Kentucky State College.]

1927: Harold Bauer & Osip Gabrilowitsch (2-piano), Fritz Kreisler.

Letter from Eugene Goossens, 1932

My dear Mrs. Salterkoff-

I understand that the pianist Dorothy Slatzenbach Payne is under consideration as soloist at the St. Louis Summer Symphony Concerts.

I am glad to hear this, for I can testify to the great success she scored with our orchestra at a Popular Concert here under my baton some four seasons ago. She has an extensive repertoire at her command, and can certainly be relied upon to give a brilliant performance in every way. I think I can safely say that she scored almost the biggest triumph of any soloist during the past five seasons of Popular concerts here. I refer, of course, to pianists.

Dorothy Payne is a real virtuoso of the piano. A real musician, cultured and unaffected.

Therein lies her greatest strength apart from her formidable technical equipment —

Greetings from
Yours sincerely
Eugene Goossens

Letter from Eugene Goossens, 1936

My dear Mrs. Holterhoff –

    I understand that the pianist, Dorothy Stolzenbach Payne, is under consideration as soloist at the St. Louis summer Symphony Concerts.

    I am glad to hear this for I can testify to the great success she scored with our orchestra at a Popular Concert here under my baton some four seasons ago. She has an extensive repertoire at her command, and can certainly be relied upon to give a brilliant performance in every way. I think I can safely say that she scores almost the biggest triumph of any soloist during the past five seasons of Popular concerts here. I refer, of course, to pianists.

    Dorothy Payne is a real virtuoso of the piano. A <u>real</u> musician, cultured and unaffected.

    Therein lies her greatest strength, apart from her formidable technical equipment –

              Greetings from

                   Yours sincerely

                   Eugene Goossens

Letter from Percy Grainger, 1959

July 15, 1959

From
Percy Grainger
7 Cromwell Place
White Plains, N. Y.
Cunard Line
R.M.S. "Queen Elizabeth"

My dear Dorothy

We had to give up our plans to go to Sweden (very reluctantly) because my left leg got so sore I could not lift it. So we thought it best to return to White Plains where my doctors know my case. In the mean time we cared the leg with hot water bottle treatment!

I took over to England Burnett Cross's recording of you & me playing on 2 pianos:

Fauré: Last movement, piano & string 4tet.
The Warriors, edition for 2 pianos s(3 pianists)
When the world was young, 2 pianos.

My musical friends (Cyril Scott, etc.) were <u>enchanted</u> with our beautiful playing of these numbers. I wish we could get more careful recordings of these things — perhaps

136

Letter from Percy Grainger, 1959, cont.

Burnett Cross could come to Cincinnati & record them for us? Or perhaps you know someone in Cinc. who takes tape recordings? I was amazed how well these 1952 recordings sound. You are a magnificent musician, & you make everything sound so well & beautifully balanced.

When you get to know more or less which days we should reserve for classes, lessons, rehearsals, etc. please kindly let me know, so I can set aside plenty of time for everything.

Ella joins in love to you all.
Thanks for your stunning playing

Yr ever
Percy

Letter from Percy Grainger, 1959

July 15, 1959

My dear Dorothy

We had to give up our plans to go to Sweden (very reluctantly) because my left leg got so sore I could not lift it. Some thought it best to return to White Plains where my doctors know my case. In the mean time we cured the leg with hot water bath treatment!

I took over to England Burnett Cross's* recording of you & me playing on 2 pianos:
Faure: Last movement, piano & string 4tet
The Warriors, edition for 2 pianos (3 pianists)
When the world was young, 2 pianos.

My musical friends (Cyril Scott, etc.) were <u>enchanted</u> with our beautiful playing of these numbers. I wish we could get more careful recordings of these things – perhaps Burnett Cross could come to Cincinnati and record them for us? Or perhaps you know someone in Cinc. who takes tape recordings? I was amazed how well these 1952 recordings sound. You are a magnificent musician, & you make everything sound so well & beautifully balanced.

When you get to know more or less which days we should reserve for classes, lessons, rehearsals, etc. please kindly let me know, so I can set aside plenty of time for anything.**

Ella joins in love to you all,

Thanks for your stunning playing

Yours ever

Percy

*Note: Burnet Cross was a physicist and good friend of Grainger's who assisted him in experiments to develop new instruments for performing new types of music (microtonal music, etc.). These included a wind instrument powered by a vacuum cleaner, but Mother said that the noise of the vacuum cleaner drowned out the music, so the project was abandoned.

**Mother had hoped to schedule another visit by Grainger to Cincinnati for a concert and master classes, but his declining health made that impossible. He passed away in February 1961.

APPENDIX III – SELECTED PHOTOS

Dorothy Payne, 1930

Dorothy Payne, 1934

Dorothy Payne, 1946

Dorothy Payne in home studio, 1967

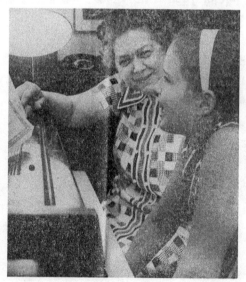

Dorothy Payne and student, 1970

Keyboard Club Meeting, ca.1970

Vronsky and Babin

Vronsky and Babin's hands

Vronsky and Babin Master Class, Home of Dick and Pinney Deupree, 1969

Payne Family Photos

Fred, Dorothy, and Margaret Stolzenbach, 1955

Karl Payne Jr.

Becky, Karl Sr., Dorothy, Karl Jr., 1962

Dorothy and Mother sailing to England, 1969

Mother, Dorothy and Karl at Becky and John's Wedding, 1970

Becky and Dorothy with Martin and Eliza Shockley, Colorado, 1980

Dorothy and Becky, Colorado, 1980

John and Becky, 1986

Karl, Susan, and Dawk, 2010

Karl, Susan, Becky and Dorothy, Minneapolis, 2002

Becky, Karl and Dorothy, Minneapolis, 2002

DeeDee Uhle, Stephanie Sepate, Karl, Terry Granick,
Bob Conda, Becky, and Rob Feldhaus
Fall Keyboard Club Recital
Wyoming Presbyterian Church, 2017

Mrs. James Werner, 1984 May Festival Chair, with John Eiden, Spencer Liles and Dorothy Payne at Opening Night.